Mission of Folly

When it is viewed that economic/ political interests could be @ risk — western forces intervene — debatable whether they intervene ble of human security — This is more of a guise to garner support & increase public opinion polls

- most always alterior motives
eg) — Afghanistan — access to oil & natural gas Pipeline
 — natural resources & geopolitics
- Haiti — suppressed the rise of a potential influencial social leader

JAMES LAXER

MISSION OF FOLLY

CANADA AND AFGHANISTAN

BETWEEN THE LINES

Toronto

Mission of Folly: Canada and Afghanistan

© 2008 by James Laxer

First published in 2008 by
Between the Lines
720 Bathurst Street, Suite #404
Toronto, Ontario M5S 2R4
Canada
1-800-718-7201
www.btlbooks.com

Library and Archives Canada Cataloguing in Publication

Laxer, James, 1941–
    Mission of folly : Canada and Afghanistan / James Laxer.

Includes index.
ISBN 978-1-897071-37-3

    1.Afghan War, 2001– —Participation, Canadian. 2.Canada—Armed Forces—
Afghanistan. 3.Canada—Military policy. 4.Canada—Foreign relations—1945– 5.United
States—Foreign relations—2001–. I.Title.
DS371.412.L39 2008   958.104'7   C2008-901354-9

Cover and text design by David Vereschagin, Quadrat Communications
Printed in Canada

Between the Lines gratefully acknowledges assistance for its publishing activities from the
Canada Council for the Arts, the Ontario Arts Council, the Government of Ontario through
the Ontario Book Publishers Tax Credit program and through the Ontario Book Initiative, and the Government of Canada through the Book Publishing Industry Development
Program.

To the memory of my father, Robert M. Laxer, who during the Second World War served overseas as a First Lieutenant in the Royal Canadian Artillery.

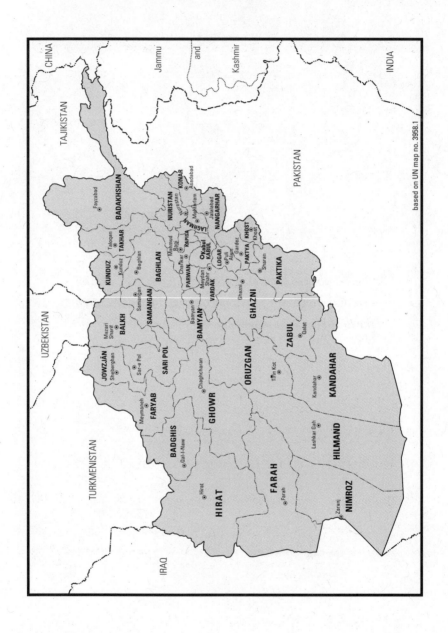

based on UN map no. 3958.1

Contents

Acknowledgements

I am much indebted to those at Between the Lines who took on this project with enthusiasm, lending me much needed support in the process. Thanks to Paul Eprile who suggested the publication of *Mission of Folly* as a book.

Robert Clarke did a masterful job editing the manuscript. I very much enjoyed working with him.

I am grateful to Jane Springer, who read the manuscript and offered advice. Thanks to my literary agent Jackie Kaiser for her role in making this book happen.

As with my other books, my spouse, Sandy, did more than her share in discussions of the issues and ideas that are the subject matter here.

1

Canada in Afghanistan: War First, Rationale Later

THE CANADIAN MILITARY MISSION IN AFGHANISTAN
was launched during the fevered weeks that followed the terror attacks
on New York City and Washington D.C. on September 11, 2001—and
the government of Jean Chrétien rather casually took the decision to
fight. The members of the Liberal cabinet saw the commitment as a
way of showing solidarity with the Americans at a time of almost universal sympathy for the United States internationally and certainly in
Canada. But the decision-making process ignored the experts in the
Canadian Forces. The government had no real idea how many soldiers
could be sent, equipped, and sustained in the field in Afghanistan. The
little advice that the government did receive from the top soldiers was
that anything beyond a token commitment would be very expensive
and would soon strain the Canadian Forces, making it difficult to meet
their existing commitments.

When politicians plunge their nations into war, they generally
have their eyes on recent conflicts as a guide to what can be expected.

For Canada, the two most recent military outings prior to Afghanistan were the Kosovo conflict and the first Gulf War. Both were short affairs, decisively won by the side on which Canada fought. It was natural enough for Chrétien and his advisors to assume that the Afghanistan war would be over or nearly over before many Canadians saw action. During the weeks when British prime minister Tony Blair emerged as the great friend of America and Chrétien had not yet visited Ground Zero in New York, the gesture was the thing. The military mission came first, the rationale later.

In the years that have passed since that gesture was made, Canada's Afghan mission has morphed into something that its initiators did not anticipate. For a time this involvement suited the Liberal government to a T. When the Bush administration launched its invasion of Iraq in March 2003, Canada was locked into the Afghanistan operation. Chrétien's announcement in the House of Commons that Canada would not join the "coalition of the willing" in its assault on Iraq drew a sustained cheer from the Liberal caucus in parliament.[1] That moment is now seen as a crucial juncture in the evolution of Canadian foreign policy. When Liberals are called upon to justify themselves to the nation, they point to the refusal to join the invasion of Iraq as their finest hour. Nonetheless, the Canadian Afghan operation could be presented to the Bush administration as proof of the devotion of the Chrétien government to the global War on Terror.

The election of Stephen Harper's Conservative government in the winter of 2006 changed the tone of Canadian foreign policy. While the Liberals had found comfort in the ambiguity of their position—out of Iraq, but in Afghanistan—the Conservatives sought no such ambiguity.

Well before becoming prime minister, Harper had served notice that if elected he would preside over the most pro-American government in Canadian history. During the time when the Liberal government was refusing to join the "coalition of the willing," Harper was attending pro-Iraq war rallies, making it clear that if he were prime minister he would join in the fight.

As Opposition leader, during question period in the House of Commons, on March 25, 2003, a few days after the U.S. invasion of Iraq, Harper launched a broadside against Prime Minister Chrétien on the issue of Iraq:

> The anti-American remarks from the government have not gone unnoticed, neither has its failure to stand by our friends and allies.
>
> Today, the American ambassador stated that the United States would stand behind Canada in a crisis without debate and without hesitation, and he asked why we are not doing the same for our friends now.
>
> When will the government do the right thing and back our American friends and allies because, frankly sir, you are embarrassing us.[2]

By the time Harper did become prime minister, as leader of a fragile minority government he fully recognized that to advocate participation in the war in Iraq—a war, by then, highly unpopular in the United States—would be unthinkable in Canada. Instead Harper injected the pent-up pro-war enthusiasm of his party into the Afghanistan mission.

3

Far from being a Liberal alibi for non-involvement in Iraq, Afghanistan became the place in which a neo-conservative Canada could make its mark.

Earlier, in the autumn of 2001, there had been no parliamentary vote to authorize what would turn out to be Canada's bloodiest military engagement since Korea. In October 2001 Canadian parliamentarians engaged in a "take note" debate, a debate structured so as not to result in a vote in the House of Commons. During the debate, the Chrétien government declared that Canada would participate in Operation Apollo, the codename—derived from the U.S. moon landing project—for the mission of Canadian military units in support of the U.S. invasion of Afghanistan. The technique of using a take note debate to commit Canada to a foreign operation was not a new one—the Chrétien government had introduced its use in 1994. It is a method providing a soupçon of parliamentary participation that leaves the real decision squarely in the hands of the prime minister and his cabinet. Take note debates were held in 1998 and 1999 at the time of Canada's commitment of fighter planes to participate in the Kosovo conflict.

Over many decades Canada's record of holding full debates about important military commitments has been shockingly poor. In the case of the Korean conflict in the early 1950s, the Liberal government of Louis St. Laurent simply announced that Canada would participate in what it called the "police action" in that country. Having entered the First World War in 1914 with no parliamentary vote on the grounds that "when Britain is at war, Canada is at war," Canada graduated to sovereignty in the Second World War. On September 10, 1939, a week after Britain's declaration of war, Canada declared war on Nazi

Germany following a debate and vote in parliament. Since the end of the Second World War—which involved other Canadian declarations of war—Canada has never declared war when entering a conflict.

In May 2006 the Harper government marginally improved on this shoddy record when it held a debate that ended in a vote to extend the Afghan mission by two years. Despite the vote, which passed by the narrow margin of 149 to 145 in the House of Commons, the debate was rushed and perfunctory, without the benefit of serious parliamentary hearings and input.[3] MPs were notified only two days prior to the debate that it would be held, and they addressed the issue for only six hours.

For decades, then, Canadians have been poorly served by successive governments when it comes to serious public dialogue on questions of war and peace. Decisions about foreign policy and war need to be thoroughly opened up and democratized. Centralized government by cabinet on these issues is not good enough.

Having had no real debate on Canada's military mission in Afghanistan, Canadians have been left instead with the Harper government's threadbare rationale for the war. The government justifies the Canadian military mission in Afghanistan with two basic arguments. The first is that unless Canada and its allies prevail there, the terrorists will regroup to carry out lethal attacks against targets in Western countries, including Canada. Fight them there to avoid having to fight them here, the logic goes. The second argument is that the struggle is about the creation of a democracy in Afghanistan, a society that will be governed by the rule of law, in which human rights, in particular the rights of women, will be enshrined. Those who reject the government's position are dismissed with the epithet that they would "cut and run."

Unwilling to defend, in a rational debate, the basic propositions on which the mission is based, Harper and his foreign minister, and later defence minister, Peter MacKay, have resorted to questioning the courage of their opponents as though these critics lacked manliness.

Both of the propositions on which the government justified Canada's participation in the war in Afghanistan were, to put it politely, open to question. To put it less politely, very strong arguments can be made that they have been the exact opposite of the truth. On the first argument, a strong case can be made that it is precisely the presence of Western armies, such as Canada's, in the Middle East and Central Asia that is drawing recruits into networks whose purpose is to lash out at the West in terrorist attacks. The second argument, that this is a fight for democracy, the rule of law, and women's rights, quickly crumbles beneath any sustained look at what is actually going on in Afghanistan and how the West's mission there was conceived in the first place.

As for the government's dismissal of critics as cowards who would cut and run, this is nothing but the lowest form of wartime propaganda. The government's argument is circular. We are in Afghanistan because we are in Afghanistan. Our soldiers are fighting and dying there. To question the mission and cast it into doubt lowers the morale of our fighting men and women and gives succour to the enemy. Having had no real debate, now that we are in the fight it is unpatriotic to have a real debate.

Increasingly Canadians are insisting on an authentic national dialogue on the Afghanistan question. Many, if not most, Canadians are deeply troubled by our country's military mission in that country. Just as Americans have brushed aside the argument that to debate the war in Iraq is unpatriotic, Canadians are not impressed by flag-waving attempts to avoid debate on our Afghan mission.

In August 2007 the Angus Reid organization published a poll on the views of Canadians on the mission in Afghanistan. The question read: "Canada has contributed troops to the North Atlantic Treaty Organization (NATO) mission in Afghanistan. So far, do you think the war against militant groups in Afghanistan has been mostly a success or mostly a failure?"

Some 49 per cent of respondents said they believed the mission had been a failure, and only 22 per cent deemed it a success. Some 52 per cent of women and 46 per cent of men viewed the mission as a failure. Significantly, younger adults—aged eighteen to thirty-four—were even more inclined to see the mission as a failure. About 50 per cent of the respondents in this age group (the age group from which Canadian soldiers are drawn) said the mission had been a failure, and only 19 per cent rated it a success. A January 2008 public opinion poll found that 56 per cent of those questioned opposed Canada's role in Afghanistan; and 47 per cent said they wanted Canada's troops to return as soon as possible.[4]

Public hearings across the country and hearings before a parliamentary committee ought to precede any future vote in the House of Commons on the issue of Canada's military mission in Afghanistan. In October 2007 Prime Minister Harper gave the nation the semblance of a serious national inquiry, without the substance. He announced the formation of a five-member panel to recommend a future role for Canada in Afghanistan at the expiration of the current military commitment, which is due to end in February 2009. Chosen to head the panel was Liberal John Manley, a former deputy prime minister. The naming of Manley gave the appearance of non-partisanship, but Manley's stoutly hawkish views and his active promotion of the deep integration of Canada into an all-encompassing North American Union made him a ludicrous choice to head any panel whose views could not be predicted in advance. Manley was co-chair of the Independent Task Force on the Future of North America, a big-business lobby effort to bind Canada to the United States economically and militarily, and in a joint security agenda. The other members named by Harper to the panel were: Derek Burney, former Canadian ambassador in Washington; broadcaster Pamela Wallin, who served as consul-general in New York; Paul Tellier, former clerk of the Privy Council; and Jake Epp, a former cabinet minister in the government of Brian Mulroney.[5] The panel was a cynical exercise in seeking "feedback" from a group that would tell the prime minister what he wanted to hear.

While it did address other issues, the main import of the Manley Report, released in January 2008, was that the Harper government should issue an ultimatum to Canada's NATO partners: that unless they send an additional thousand soldiers to Kandahar by February 2009 to help the Canadians posted there, Canada should terminate its mission in that region. Provided that these reinforcements were forthcoming, the report urged that Canada's military commitment in Afghanistan be extended indefinitely and deepened in its intensity.

The report shed little light on the conflict in Afghanistan. It is difficult to avoid the conclusion that it was written both to please the Harper government and to curry favour with the White House and Number 10 Downing Street. It appeared to be based on the dubious assumption that all political and military reality grows out of the West and ultimately the West can do what it likes in Afghanistan, if only it summons up sufficient political will.

Canadians have been subject to top-down decisions on their military and foreign policies throughout their history. In recent years there has been considerable discussion about the functioning of Canadian democracy and the existence in the country of what can be called a "democratic deficit." The most eloquent testimony to the existence of a democratic deficit is the sharp decline of the proportion of Canadians who vote in federal and provincial elections. Increasingly, Canadians believe that their votes do not matter and that politicians are more concerned with themselves than with the well-being of Canadians. This sentiment is especially pronounced among young Canadians, whose participation in elections is lower than is the case for older citizens.

Opening up the way in which Canada debates military missions and foreign policy can be efficacious in improving the functioning of our democracy. Decisions taken by those at the centre of government, with little or no consultation, can have an especially onerous impact on young Canadians. Public discourse about whether Canada ought to send troops to a country on the other side of the world rarely focuses on who will actually be sent to do the fighting and stand in harm's way. It is, of course, the young, who are recruited by government advertising directed especially at those who have relatively few attractive economic options. While plenty of attention has been paid in the media to the troops already in Afghanistan or about to go to Afghanistan, and the risks they face, little discussion has taken place about how privileged people in an older generation make life and death decisions about the young people recruited into the Canadian Forces.

Here are some of the questions that need to be addressed in a national debate about the war in Afghanistan, among Canadians at large as well as in Parliament.

- What is the purpose of the Canadian military mission in Afghanistan? How do we define success?
- What is the balance in the mission between making war on the insurgents and aiding in the process of reconstructing a country that has been torn by war for decades?
- Is a proportionate military effort being made by other NATO countries?
- What role is Pakistan playing in the conflict?
- Now that the United States is rethinking its mission in Iraq, is it likely to remain committed to a long-term military effort in Afghanistan?
- How many Canadian lives are we prepared to sacrifice in this conflict?
- Does the Canadian mission in Afghanistan make Canada a more or less likely target of terrorism?
- Can foreign armies in Afghanistan advance the cause of democracy, the rule of law, and human rights, or does their presence undermine these goals by drawing recruits, in the region as well as in the West, into the ranks of the Muslim fundamentalists?

Canadians need a wide-ranging national dialogue—one that we have not had to date—on whether our country's military mission in Afghanistan is right for our country. Politicians need to play a candid role in this dialogue, but so too does the general public. This is not a debate for the experts. We all have a stake in how it turns out. Indeed, when it comes to the experts Canadians have, with a few notable exceptions, been ill-served by the mainstream media on the Afghanistan question. There has been shockingly little analytical journalism on this war, its origins and course, and the role Canada is playing in it. Too much of the reportage has come from journalists embedded with the Canadian Forces; their stories are like those of sports writers working for the home team.

The national conversation should focus on the specifics of Canada's Afghan mission. It must consider as well the wider military and political struggles that are unfolding in the Middle East and Central Asia. Afghanistan is but one theatre in that much larger struggle. What happens elsewhere, particularly in Iraq, is bound to have a significant impact on the fate of the NATO mission in Afghanistan and, therefore, on the Canadian mission in that country. Moreover, the debate will be incomplete unless it also considers the broad goals of Canadian foreign and military policy.

■ ■

Need a national conversation/debate that is inclusive of the public.

2

The Invasion and Occupation

OPERATION ENDURING FREEDOM, THE U.S. ASSAULT ON Afghanistan, commenced on October 7, 2001, almost four weeks after the terror attacks on New York City and Washington, D.C. Initial aerial attacks were carried out by land-based B-1, B-2, and B-52 bombers, as well as by carrier-based F-14 and F/A-18 bombers. In addition Tomahawk cruise missiles were launched at enemy targets from U.S. and British ships.[1]

The goals of the Afghanistan mission were outlined to the U.S. Congress and to the American people in two speeches delivered by President George W. Bush. The first address, to the U.S. Congress, introduced the weighty rationale of a new War on Terror. The second, a live television address to the people of the United States, explained the purposes of the U.S. assault on Afghanistan.

"The evidence we have gathered," Bush reported to Congress on September 20 in answer to the question on the minds of Americans— Who attacked the United States?—"all points to a collection of loosely affiliated terrorist organizations known as al Qaeda. They are the same murderers indicted for bombing American embassies in Tanzania and Kenya, and responsible for the bombing of the USS Cole. Al Qaeda is to terror what the mafia is to crime. But its goal is not making money; its goal is remaking the world—and imposing its radical beliefs on people everywhere."[2]

The president issued an ultimatum to the Taliban rulers of Afghanistan:

> The United States of America makes the following demands on the Taliban: Deliver to United States authorities all the leaders of al Qaeda who hide in your land. Release all foreign nationals— including American citizens—you have unjustly imprisoned, and protect foreign journalists, diplomats, and aid workers in your country. Close immediately and permanently every terrorist training camp in Afghanistan and hand over every terrorist, and every person in their support structure, to appropriate authorities. Give the United States full access to terrorist training camps, so we can make sure they are no longer operating. These demands are not open to negotiation or discussion. The Taliban must act and act immediately. They will hand over the terrorists, or they will share in their fate.

This ultimatum, a sure precursor to war, was followed by an explanation to Americans and the world that the United States was now involved in a War on Terror. Bush depicted the enemy in this wide-ranging struggle in the following terms:

Our war on terror begins with al Qaeda, but it does not end there. It will not end until every terrorist group of global reach has been found, stopped, and defeated. Americans are asking: Why do they hate us? They hate what we see right here in this chamber—a democratically elected government. Their leaders are self-appointed. They hate our freedoms—our freedom of religion, our freedom of speech, our freedom to vote and assemble and disagree with each other. They want to overthrow existing governments in many Muslim countries, such as Egypt, Saudi Arabia, and Jordan. They want to drive Israel out of the Middle East. They want to drive Christians and Jews out of vast regions of Asia and Africa.

Having issued an ultimatum to the Taliban, Bush concluded his speech with an ultimatum to the rest of the world:

Every nation, in every region, now has a decision to make. Either you are with us, or you are with the terrorists. From this day forward, any nation that continues to harbor or support terrorism will be regarded by the United States as a hostile regime.... The hour is coming when America will act.... This is not, however, just America's fight. And what is at stake is not just America's freedom. This is the world's fight. This is civilization's fight. This is the fight of all who believe in progress and pluralism, tolerance and freedom. We ask every nation to join us. We will ask, and we will need, the help of police forces, intelligence services, and banking systems around the world.

For the Bush administration, this was the seminal moment. The War on Terror would be prosecuted as a global struggle, and the United States was putting all the countries of the world on notice. There were to be no neutrals in this struggle: countries that were not on the side of the United States would be deemed to be on the side of the terrorists.

In his television address on October 7, Bush announced that the assault on the Taliban regime and al Qaeda had commenced:

> The United States military has begun strikes against al Qaeda terrorist training camps and military installations of the Taliban regime in Afghanistan. These carefully targeted actions are designed to disrupt the use of Afghanistan as a terrorist base of operations, and to attack the military capability of the Taliban regime. We are joined in this operation by our staunch friend, Great Britain. Other close friends, including Canada, Australia, Germany and France, have pledged forces as the operation unfolds. More than 40 countries in the Middle East, Africa, Europe and across Asia have granted air transit or landing rights. Many more have shared intelligence. We are supported by the collective will of the world.[3]

Bush went on to say that the goal of the military action was to drive the terrorists from their hiding places and bring them to justice. Again the president warned the nations of the world that this struggle extended far beyond Afghanistan: "Every nation has a choice to make. In this conflict, there is no neutral ground. If any government sponsors the outlaws and killers of innocents, they have become outlaws and murderers, themselves. And they will take that lonely path at their own peril."

In the style that was to characterize the global policies of his administration, Bush depicted the struggle ahead in terms of black and white, good and evil. The suffering and anguish of Americans as a consequence of September 11 were enormous, but many other countries had also directly experienced the scourge of terrorism. For years the British had lived with bombings and casualties that resulted from the campaign waged by the Irish Republican Army and its offshoots to make Northern Ireland a part of the Irish Republic. Similarly, France had suffered as a consequence of bombings perpetrated by terrorists of North African origin. In September 1986, in one episode, the Tati Department Store in Paris was attacked, resulting in seven deaths and fifty-four injuries. Most of the victims were mothers and children. Canadians had endured the Air India bombing, when, on June 23, 1985, Air India Flight 182 was blown out of the sky south of Ireland above the Atlantic Ocean. All of the 329 passengers and crew died; eighty-two were children, and 280 were Canadian citizens.[4] On a per capita basis, the Air India bombing was as devastating a blow to Canada as the September 11 attacks were to the United States.

Canada, of course, did not consider taking military action in response to the Air India bombing. It and the other countries subjected to terrorist attack mobilized the means available to them to increase their security and to guard against future attacks. The difference between the United States and the other countries that have been victims of terrorism is that the United States is uniquely powerful militarily. Alone among the countries of the world, the United States had the military means to reach out across thousands of kilometres to carry out an assault on remote Afghanistan. By deciding on a military invasion as the American response to the terror attacks, the Bush administration was raising the stakes enormously. This was no mere police action. The invasion would turf out the regime in power and replace it with another; and by declaring that the action in Afghanistan was only one front in a much wider War on Terror in which the whole world was involved, the Bush administration was raising the stakes much further still. The United States was pledging to deliver its version of liberty to humanity and to rid the world of a dark menace.

From the beginning the Afghan mission, Operation Enduring Freedom—the U.S. name for the assault—was cast in ideological terms. Its authors would not be satisfied with success against the Taliban and al Qaeda camps in Afghanistan. They were determined to use the provocation of September 11 to change the world and to increase the power of the United States throughout the globe. Pentagon planners complained that Afghanistan had precious few military targets of high value. While Afghanistan was the immediate target, from the first days the top decision-makers in the administration were thinking about a showdown with what they regarded as a much more important foe, Iraq. Even before the invasion of Afghanistan, Vice-President Dick Cheney, Defense Secretary Donald Rumsfeld, and Undersecretary of Defense Paul Wolfowitz were preoccupied with the idea of an invasion of Iraq. In their thinking, Iraq would be the decisive field of battle; Afghanistan was merely the sideshow.

The coming assault on Iraq was the focal point of U.S. foreign policy and military policy from the earliest days after September 11. The neo-conservatives who dominated the Bush administration developed a theory about how an American occupation of Iraq would lead to positive results for the United States on a number of crucial issues in the Middle East. The assumption on which the earlier administration of George Bush Sr. had operated was that to improve the U.S. position in the Middle East, the Palestinian question would have to be settled. The administration of George W. Bush started from a radically different premise—that a U.S. occupation of Iraq would open the door to a settlement of the Palestinian question that would suit both Israel and the United States.

The idea, advanced by Wolfowitz, was that if the United States occupied Iraq and ushered a pro-American regime into power, Iraq could develop into a model democratic, constitutional state in which Islam was the religion of the population but radical Islamic theocratic concepts could be pushed to the margin. Iraq would be America's tabula rasa in the region, the blank slate on which the United States could write its liberal-democratic narrative. The effect would reverberate through the region.

Other benefits would accrue to the United States from the occupation of Iraq. Bordering on Saudi Arabia, Iran, and Syria, Iraq would be an ideal place for the U.S. government to establish permanent military bases. The Saudis were prickly about the political effects of having U.S. forces stationed on their territory. From Iraq the United States would be able to keep a close eye on the hostile regimes in Iran and Syria. U.S. power in the Persian Gulf would be ensured. The United States would be able to establish a dominant position for its oil companies in Iraq and look out for their interests in the rest of the Middle East. In addition, a strengthened position in the region would help muscle the Palestinians into taking what they could get in a deal with Israel, even if it fell far short of creating a state on all of the territory that Israel had occupied since 1967, including East Jerusalem.

These were heady dreams, no less than a utopian vision for the political transformation of a major region of the world, and they were to morph into nightmares. The details of the U.S.-led invasion of Iraq are well known and need not detain us here. What is significant is how that invasion turned out.

On May 1, 2003, weeks after the U.S. assault on Iraq, President Bush landed in a warplane on the deck of the USS *Abraham Lincoln*.[5] After the tailhook landing, he climbed out of the plane, greeted by a huge banner that read "mission accomplished." Dressed in the fatigues of a Navy fighter pilot, Bush swaggered across the deck. The president, who had avoided combat in Vietnam as a member of the Texas Air National Guard, was presiding over a quickly won military triumph, or so it seemed.

Flash forward to November 7, 2006. With U.S. combat deaths in Iraq approaching 3,000, with dead and wounded together exceeding 25,000, and with Iraq sinking into civil war, U.S. voters handed both houses of Congress to the Democrats. The day after the election, Defense Secretary Rumsfeld resigned. His designated replacement, Robert Gates, in a congressional confirmation hearing, frankly acknowledged that the United States was not winning in Iraq. On December 6, 2006, the Iraq Study Group, headed by Republican James Baker and Democrat Lee Hamilton, reported its recommendations to the

Bush administration.[6] Established to find a way of getting the United States out of the Iraq quagmire, the Study Group's recommendations amounted to a flat repudiation of the foreign and military policies of the administration. The report recommended the withdrawal of large numbers of U.S. forces from Iraq by the beginning of 2008 and advised that overtures be made to Syria and Iran to seek the collaboration of these countries in finding a settlement of the conflict in Iraq.

Almost from the first days of the U.S. assault, Afghanistan became the forgotten war. Always the centre of the American strategic effort in the Middle East and Central Asia, Iraq continued to condition the outcome of the struggle in Afghanistan. If the United States were to withdraw in disgrace from Iraq (now the most likely outcome), it was exceedingly unlikely that the United States would commit to a lengthy war in Afghanistan.

■ ■

During the first phase of the assault on Afghanistan, the Americans operated with impunity in the air, concentrating their attacks on Kabul, Kandahar, and Jalalabad as well as on al Qaeda training camps. The Taliban quickly lost their ability to co-ordinate their efforts, with their systems of "command and control" rapidly degraded.

The Americans and their allies were not the only opponents of the Taliban. The regime in Kabul was already in a state of conflict with a force called the Northern Alliance (also known as the United Front) when the U.S. attack began. The Northern Alliance was composed of diverse ethnic and religious elements whose members, for one reason or another, were involved in an insurgency against the Taliban. While the power of the Taliban rested largely on the Pashtuns, who predominated in the country's south and east, the Northern Alliance was mainly non-Pashtun. At the time of the September 11 terror attacks, the Northern Alliance fielded a core force of about fifteen thousand soldiers, mostly Tajik and Uzbek fighters, whose base was in northeastern Afghanistan in Badakhshan, as well as in eastern Takhar province, the Panjshir Valley, and part of the Shomali plain north of Kabul.[7] The Northern Alliance counted on support from Iran, Russia, and Tajikistan.

Viewed over the longer term, the U.S. involvement in Afghanistan, which pre-dated the invasion of 2001, resembled a revolving door. Friends became foes and foes became friends in farcical fashion. When the Soviet Union invaded Afghanistan in 1979, the United States helped sponsor the creation of the Mujahideen, a fundamentalist Islamic movement that opposed the Soviets and despised the secular pro-Soviet regime in Kabul. Osama bin Laden learned much about insurgent warfare during those times, when he was on the American-backed side against the Soviets. Later, when the Soviets were driven out, subsequent struggles led to the installation of the Taliban regime, whose fighters included many who had fought on the side of those supported by Washington. Still later, when the Gulf War in 1991 involved a marked increase in the U.S. military presence in Saudi Arabia, Osama bin Laden became an embittered enemy of America. A Saudi himself, he was no more prepared to contemplate a large Infidel (American) presence in the land that housed Islam's holiest sites than he was to abide the Soviet hold on Afghanistan.

In autumn 2001, then, the Americans were attacking a country that had earlier been liberated by forces they had backed—forces that were now their enemies, while their friends numbered among them foes from the previous struggle. The rhetoric served up for Americans, Canadians, and Europeans was that this was a struggle about human rights and democracy; but the forces involved and their respective histories made this an implausible claim from the start.

On the old premise that the enemy of my enemy is my friend, the Americans saw the Northern Alliance fighters as their allies, a ready-made ground force that could make gains as the United States pounded the Taliban from the air. For the first couple of weeks, the Taliban lines held against the Northern Alliance. Then the shellacking from the air and the inexperience of Taliban fighters in the face of U.S. air power took effect. By early November, Taliban lines were crumbling. The Northern Alliance fighters advanced and seized the strategic city of Mazare Sharif, unleashing widespread looting and executions. Over five hundred Taliban soldiers, many of them from Pakistan, were massacred after being found hiding in a school.

The seizure of Mazare Sharif triggered a collapse of the Taliban regime, not only in the north, but also in the south. On November 12 the Taliban fled Kabul, and the capital was occupied the next day by the Northern Alliance. Over the next day or two the Taliban regime collapsed virtually everywhere outside its southeastern stronghold of Kandahar. Pashtun warlords seized control in large parts of the country's northeast, including the city of Jalalabad.

On the run, the remaining Taliban and al Qaeda forces, most likely including Osama bin Laden, fell back on the cave complex of Tora Bora, next to the Pakistan border, southwest of Jalalabad. As U.S. aerial attacks and Northern Alliance fighters sealed the fate of the city of Konduz, the Pakistani air force sent in aircraft to evacuate intelligence and military personnel who had entered Afghanistan in alliance with the Taliban and al Qaeda. As many as five thousand people were evacuated from the region by the Pakistanis. Pakistan's ties with the Taliban and al Qaeda were a factor in the Afghanistan situation prior to September 11 and the subsequent American attack. Pakistan has remained a key player there during the subsequent five years.

With U.S. ground forces joining the struggle, the battle for Kandahar got underway, as did an American assault on the fighters in the caves of Tora Bora. On December 7, Mullah Omar, the leader of the Taliban, recognized the hopelessness of his position in Kandahar and escaped from the city as the Americans closed in on the airport and Afghan tribal forces seized the city. A few days later, U.S. Special Forces units and their Afghan allies fought for control of the caves of Tora Bora, backed up by U.S. air power. The Taliban and al Qaeda fighters managed a delaying action to allow top al Qaeda leaders, possibly including Osama bin Laden, to escape into border regions of Pakistan to the south and east.[8] (The Americans have proved unsuccessful in hunting down bin Laden, just as their forebears were unsuccessful in their pursuit of Pancho Villa when the United States invaded northern Mexico in 1916.)

By the end of December 2001, the largely conventional phase of the war was over. At that point victory appeared to be in the grasp of the Americans and their Afghan allies. As with previous invasions of Afghanistan, however, those events were only the beginning. That same month Afghan political leaders who had opposed the Taliban met in Bonn, Germany, to draw up plans for the installation of a new regime. An Interim Transitional Administration was created. Named chairman of a twenty-nine-member body was Hamid Karzai, who was also appointed to the position of leader on December 22. Six months later, he was appointed interim president of the transitional administration.

Originally a supporter of the Taliban, Karzai, born in Kandahar, was a member of a prominent Pashtun family. When the Taliban took power in 1996, driving the regime of Burhanuddin Rabbani out of office, Karzai, who had formerly served as a deputy foreign minister, refused to serve as the UN ambassador of the new government. He withdrew to Quetta, Pakistan, where he advocated the restoration of the Afghan monarchy. In July 1999 Karzai's father was assassinated, a killing that has been attributed to the Taliban. Following the murder Karzai threw himself into the struggle against the Taliban.

As interim president of the new Afghan regime, Karzai exercised little real authority. He earned the nickname "Mayor of Kabul" from those who made the point that outside the capital real power was exercised by warlords and tribal regional authorities. Though limited in his capacity to govern, Karzai nonetheless became extremely well known internationally. The Bush administration adopted him as the face of the new, and supposedly democratic, Afghanistan. The Karzai regime was touted as being committed to the rights of women, a major selling point in contrasting it to the Taliban's harshly repressive policies.[9]

In October 2004, nationwide elections were held in Afghanistan. With his high name-recognition, the open backing of the Bush administration, and the use of U.S. army transport during his election campaign, Karzai emerged first among the twenty-three candidates for the office of president. With 55.4 per cent of the 8.1 million votes cast, Karzai was declared elected without the need for a second run-off ballot. At his swearing-in ceremony in December 2004, the former Afghan king and U.S. vice-president Dick Cheney were present.[10]

While the new U.S.-backed regime of Hamid Karzai was working to secure its legitimacy throughout the country, an increasingly potent insurgency was mounted against it. The Taliban had been beaten in the short military campaign in the autumn of 2001, but now the organization was back, with new allies and fighting a very different kind of war. These foes of the U.S. occupation of the country and of the new regime in Kabul soon learned how to wage a guerrilla war, and they were able to capitalize on the estrangement of very large parts of the country from the new government. The assumption that the Taliban was beaten—sold to the outside world by the Bush administration, and by photo ops of Karzai with foreign leaders in Kabul—turned out to be as false as Bush's spring 2003 claim that the American mission in Iraq had been accomplished.

U.S. and allied Afghan forces continued to mount large-scale operations against the Taliban and al Qaeda insurgents, such as Operation Anaconda in March 2002. In that operation, hundreds of insurgent fighters were killed, but hundreds more managed to slip back across the border into Pakistan. Pakistani forces, who were supposed to seal off the border against just such an escape, proved unwilling or unable to carry out their task.

By summer 2002 the insurgents were carrying out highly effective raids against U.S. forces and their Afghan and other allies. In bands numbering from five to twenty-five men, the insurgents moved quickly, blending effectively into the local population and assaulting their opponents with mobile rocket attacks. Hit and run tactics allowed them to inflict casualties against the much better armed Americans and their allies.

In its ancient and modern forms, insurgent warfare combines military and political elements that make life extremely difficult for an occupying force. Foreign occupying armies, however mighty their weaponry, suffer from their lack of knowledge of the local population. They don't speak the language, they are remote from the culture and customs of the people, and they stand out as aliens in the landscape, no matter how many candy bars they dispense or children's soccer matches they organize. Insurgents speak the language and follow up their attacks by fleeing into villages, where they look like members of the local population. Insurgent tactics are designed precisely to heighten the perception in the population that the occupiers are to be feared, and that they are the source of the country's problems.

The insurgents' hit and run attacks have the natural and intended effect of making the soldiers of the occupying armies ever more fearful and hostile, towards not only the guerrilla warriors, but the local population as well. Sudden attacks in villages and towns, inflicted by men in civilian clothes, riding bicycles or suddenly appearing in the midst of crowds, force a change in tactics by the occupiers. They have to set up roadblocks and checkpoints to keep people at arm's-length, and to sort them out, before letting them go about their business. They issue orders to people to stop when commanded to do so and open fire when they do not.

And then there are the tragic errors when trigger-happy soldiers kill innocent people who fail to stop at checkpoints, and top-gun pilots blow up celebrants at wedding parties. These atrocities reinforce the growing antagonism of the population towards the occupiers. The antagonism generates a spiral that strengthens the insurgency and makes the task of soldiers who are far from home ever more difficult.

In the autumn of 2002 the Taliban launched a major recruiting drive centred on the Pashtun areas in the south and southeast. In this jihad, whose purpose was to drive the foreigners out of Afghanistan, the Taliban also drew in recruits from the Pakistani side of the border, particularly young men who had attended the *madrassas*, religious schools that honed the ideology of resistance. Taliban and al Qaeda fighters set up small training camps in border areas, and on the Pakistan side of the border they created encampments with as many as two hundred men each. Despite the supposed commitment of the government of Pakistan to the War on Terror, the Taliban and al Qaeda faced few problems from the local Pakistani forces.

Like everything else in this war, reality and public rhetoric had little to do with one another. The fighters on the side of the United States, including President Karzai, had little commitment to the human rights cause that was so widely trumpeted by the Bush administration. They ended up on the U.S. side for reasons that mostly had to do with tribal loyalties, regional and personal power struggles, and mere chance. The fighters on the other side were similarly drawn into the struggle for a wide variety of reasons. Devotion to the ideology of the Taliban or al Qaeda was only one of them. Tribal loyalties, personal grudges, antagonism against the foreign invaders, and anger at efforts to shut down the lucrative poppy trade, the source of 90 per cent of the world's heroin, were others.

With a new command structure under the overall leadership of Mullah Omar, a ten-man leadership council was created to co-ordinate the Taliban insurgency. Signs of the new organizational structure were evident by January 2003. In summer 2003 hit and run attacks in the Taliban heartland of the southeast and major operations in the mountains next to the Pakistan border were launched. The war that the Americans thought they had won nearly two years earlier had returned with a vengeance.

In 2005 and 2006 the United States and its allies, including Canada, struck back at the Taliban with major offensives designed to deny them any ability to hold territory and to cut down on the number of fighters they could deploy. Despite the intensification of the allied effort, by July 2006 British commanders in Afghanistan were warning Prime Minister Blair that the war was far from won. A study undertaken by the British Royal Statistical Society concluded that during the period from May 1, 2006, to August 12, 2006, an average of five allied soldiers were killed each week by the insurgents, which was twice the rate of casualties suffered by the Americans and their allies weekly during the invasion of Iraq in 2003.[11]

On October 5, 2006, when twelve thousand U.S. troops came under its sway, NATO assumed overall control of allied operations in all regions of Afghanistan, with British Lieutenant-General David Richards in command. About eight thousand U.S. troops remained under a separate U.S. command assigned with the tasks of training Afghan troops and carrying out anti-terrorist operations aimed at rounding up Taliban leaders and al Qaeda units.[12]

In the opening months of 2007 the pertinent question was how many casualties NATO countries were prepared to take to win the struggle in Afghanistan. That the United States and its allies were regularly killing Taliban and al Qaeda fighters in far greater numbers than the insurgents were inflicting deaths on them was not unimportant, but it was not decisive. Western countries are highly sensitive to the number of casualties suffered by their forces overseas. If the Taliban could continue killing enemy soldiers at a steady rate, that would become an important political fact in countries where the public was already highly sceptical about the Afghan war.

In U.S. strategic thinking, the Afghan and Iraq missions were inseparably linked. Both invasions were undertaken by the Bush administration in the belief that the United States would soon overwhelm the local forces and establish pro-American regimes that would have the support of most of the populations of the two countries. This is precisely where the Americans made their crucial miscalculation.

The U.S. military had been redesigned to make use of its superior firepower and logistical superiority to smash any foe, with a deployment of relatively small American forces. The invasions, in both cases, worked well enough, with the armies of the Taliban and Saddam Hussein rapidly overwhelmed. What the Americans did not foresee was the extent to which Afghans and Iraqis, of various sects and persuasions, would coalesce around the basic goal of pushing out the invaders. The Bush administration made the case that the insurgencies that broke out in both countries in the aftermath of the invasions were largely the work of outsiders and Islamic fundamentalists operating under the broad direction of al Qaeda. What the administration did not want to acknowledge was that the cement that held the insurgencies together was Afghan and Iraqi nationalism, the desire of very important elements in both countries not to have their futures determined by outside invaders. It was the U.S. occupation of Afghanistan and Iraq that was both the problem and the source of the resistance.

Powerfully reinforcing the antagonism of many Afghans towards the occupation has been the steady toll of civilian casualties as a consequence of the conflict. While the Taliban has certainly been responsible for civilian deaths, especially as a result of suicide attacks, the killing of innocents by the Americans and their allies provokes enormous hostility. Afghan civilians have died in U.S. air assaults that have gone astray, at checkpoints, in raids that targeted the wrong people, and in villages and towns where NATO forces have used heavy weapons to attack Taliban fighters and other insurgents. In other cases, U.S. and allied forces have raided villages, breaking into houses, tying up and subduing terrified civilians, and sometimes even killing them. Since the start of the war, the Pentagon and NATO officials have had to admit that such atrocities do occur and they are investigating them. On January 10, 2007, for instance, NATO officials in Brussels admitted that about thirty civilians had been recently killed as a result of "poor communications" between NATO troops and Afghan authorities in southern Kandahar province. Afghan officials put the number of civilians who died in the incident at up to eighty.

From the beginning there have been repeated incidents in which civilians have lost their lives as a result of the actions of the armed forces of the United States and its allies. The list is a lengthy one, and I will cite only a few well-reported cases.

- On October 10, 2001, a mosque in Jalalabad was bombed twice, once while prayers were in progress and later when efforts were being made to remove the casualties of the first bombing. Between 15 and 70 people died in the first strike and as many as 120 in the second.[13]
- On October 21, 2001, a hospital and a mosque were bombed in Herat. While the target was about thirty metres from the hospital, about one hundred bodies were discovered in the ruins.[14]
- On December 1, 2001, bombs fell on the village of Kama Ado, killing as many as one hundred people in their houses.[15]
- On July 1, 2002, in the village of Del Rawad, a bombing raid took the lives of 46 people who were celebrants at a wedding party and wounded 117 others.[16]
- On April 9, 2003, eleven people died and one was wounded in Shkin in Paktika province when a stray American laser-guided bomb struck a house.[17]
- On January 18, 2004, four children and seven adults died in a U.S. air raid in the village of Saghatho.[18]
- On October 18, 2006, during a clash between insurgents and NATO and Afghan forces in the village of Tajikai, 200 kilometres west of Kandahar, a rocket

fired from a NATO jet killed thirteen people inside a house.[19]

The U.S. military and NATO commanders have insisted that every effort is made to prevent civilian casualties. For obvious reasons, civilian casualties are highly politicized and controversial. There are both high and low claims about how many civilians have died and about who is responsible for their deaths.

Studies of the number of civilians who died in Afghanistan in U.S. aerial attacks during the first year of fighting, 2001–02, have produced estimates that vary from one thousand to five thousand. While numbers of civilian deaths for the period 2002 to 2005 are hard to find, all sources agree that 2006 was the bloodiest year of the conflict since the period of the U.S. invasion in 2001, when civilian casualties were especially high.

A BBC news story on October 26, 2006, conveyed the anguish of those who survived air raids carried out by NATO forces. In this case, the report concerned about sixty civilian deaths in two attacks in Kandahar province. "Twenty members of my family are killed and 10 are injured," one survivor told the BBC. "The injured are in Mirwais hospital in Kandahar city and anybody can go and see them. For God's sake, come and see our situation."

Another man told the BBC that women and children were among fifteen members of his family who had been killed.[20]

In late September 2007, about five hundred Afghan citizens blocked a highway during a fierce demonstration on the outskirts of Kandahar. Some of the protesters shouted "death to Canada."[21] One man at the protest told CBC News that he had guests at his house the previous night, when soldiers burst inside and seized eight men, covering their eyes and tying their hands and feet and taking them away. Another witness said that Canadian and American soldiers conducted the raid and later killed two of the men they took with them. One protester told an interpreter for Canadian Press: "They're killing our young men. The day is not far when these innocent civilians will stand against NATO and other foreign troops." People in the crowd also directed their rage against the Karzai government for allowing foreign armies to operate in the country. They said that corrupt Afghan intelligence officers had passed on faulty information, which had led to the raid.

Independent tallies of civilian deaths compiled by the United Nations concluded that in the first six months of 2007 the insurgents killed 279 civilians; NATO and Afghan government forces killed 314.[22]

■ ■

The Canadian Mission

ON SEPTEMBER 18, 2001, LIBERAL DEFENCE MINISTER
Art Eggleton announced that Canada would participate in any actions
undertaken by the United States to retaliate against al Qaeda and the
Taliban. He said,"I think we will play a major role, a front-line role. We
will make sure that the Canadian Forces get the resources they need to
do the job. We'll stand with our allies in weeding out the perpetrators,
in destroying the organizations, wherever they may be."[1] On October 4,
in response to the terror attacks, NATO Secretary-General George Rob-
ertson announced the invocation for the first time ever of the alliance's
Article 5, which declares the alliance's commitment to regard an attack
on one member state as an attack on all. The Chrétien government
supported this step, which was advocated by the Bush administration
and Blair government.[2]

On October 7, just hours after the United States and United Kingdom launched their initial attacks on Afghanistan, Prime Minister Chrétien declared in a televised speech that Canada would be part of the U.S.-

led operation "every step of the way." He said that the United States had "asked Canada to make certain contributions as part of an international military coalition against international terrorism." He expressed his conviction that Canada's armed forces would do "Canada proud."[3] The following day, Eggleton announced the establishment of Operation Apollo. Orders were quickly dispatched to HMCS *Halifax* to sail to the Arabian Sea, where the ship would participate in Operation Enduring Freedom. Just over a week later, two more Canadian ships sailed for the combat zone, and in November a fourth ship was sent from the west coast.

Right from the start wrangling occurred within the Canadian government about the size, and the type, of the Canadian military commitment to Afghanistan. In their book *The Unexpected War: Canada in Kandahar*, published in the fall of 2007, Janice Gross Stein and Eugene Lang shed light on how power struggles in Ottawa between government departments, in addition to the Canadian-American relationship on a range of issues, affected the mission in Afghanistan from its inception to its later evolution.

Following the rout of Taliban forces in the autumn of 2001 and the establishment of an interim Afghan government in Bonn, the International Security Assistance Force (ISAF) was authorized by the passage of a United Nations Security Council resolution on December 20. The resolution was passed under the authority of chapter 7 of the UN Charter. The ISAF was not funded by the United Nations. Participating member states paid for their individual missions and mobilized their own forces to serve in them. In this sense, the ISAF was not a customary UN mission. Initially the ISAF operation was led by Britain, but in August 2003 NATO formally took over its command.

The operations of the United States and its ISAF allies were initially organized as two separate missions. The U.S. mission, Operation Enduring Freedom, was completely controlled by the United States. It comprised mostly U.S. forces and involved the participation of the forces of a few European allies, as well as some Canadians. The ISAF operation was a separate undertaking. For the first two years of its existence, forces under the ISAF were confined to providing security in Kabul and in the relatively peaceful north and west of the country. Their goal was to pacify the Afghan capital and to lend muscular support to the creation of the new Afghan government.[4] Meanwhile, the United States and other allied forces, which were under U.S. command in Operation Enduring Freedom, undertook the task of fighting the Taliban and other insurgents in the rest of the country.

Although the Canadian public did not learn of it at the time, by early December 2001 the Canadian government had secretly sent forty members of Joint Task Force 2 (JTF-2), the country's elite special forces, into southern Afghanistan near Kandahar. The unit had never before been sent abroad to engage in a combat mission. In this mission, JTF-2 served under the U.S. command in the region.[5]

Canadian forces were involved both in Operation Enduring Freedom under U.S. command and in the ISAF mission in Kabul. In mid-January 2002, twenty Canadian soldiers arrived in Kandahar as a lead group. Their task was to prepare for the arrival a few weeks later of 750 members of Princess Patricia's Canadian Light Infantry, based in Edmonton. The battle group was to serve in U.S. operations against the Taliban in the mountainous south of Afghanistan.

In spring 2002 a "friendly fire" incident, in which U.S. forces inflicted casualties on Canadian soldiers, was the first major shock of the war for the Canadian public. On April 18, 2002, in the so-called Tarnak Farm Incident, a U.S. F-16 fighter jet dropped a laser-guided bomb on a unit of Canadian soldiers. Four Canadians died: Sgt. Marc D. Leger, twenty-nine, from Lancaster, Ontario; Cpl. Ainsworth Dyer, twenty-four, from Montreal; Pt. Richard Green, twenty-one, from Mill Cove, Nova Scotia; and Pt. Nathan Smith, twenty-seven, from Porters Lake, Nova Scotia. In addition, eight Canadian soldiers were wounded. The U.S. pilot, Major William Umbach, and his wingman, Major Harry Schmidt, were responding to what they perceived as surface-to-air fire against their aircraft, but what they were really coming across was a Canadian anti-tank and machine-gun exercise. Both Canadian and U.S. military inquiries were held to investigate the incident. The report of the Canadian military board concluded that the Canadian night live-fire exercise had been properly conducted according to agreed upon procedures, and that responsibility for the incident lay with the U.S. airmen who contravened established procedures.

On September 11, 2002, the two U.S. officers were charged with four counts of negligent manslaughter, eight counts of aggravated assault, and one count of dereliction of duty. Eventually the charges against the pilot, Major Umbach, were dismissed. Those against the wingman, Major Schmidt, were reduced solely to the dereliction of duty charge. Schmidt was reprimanded and fined nearly $5,700 in pay. It was found that when he dropped the bomb, Schmidt "flagrantly disregarded a direct order" to hold fire.

The incident received enormous media attention. It left a foul taste in the mouths of Canadians, who generally believed that the U.S. pilots got off too lightly considering the gravity of the incident. The incident, which brought the war home in a visceral way to many Canadians, reinforced the sentiment that the United States always puts its own interests first, even in relations with close allies.[6]

The six-month-long mission of the soldiers of Princess Patricia's in southern Afghanistan turned out to be merely an initial deployment of Canadians in the Afghan war. In February 2003 Defence Minister John McCallum announced that Canada would send soldiers back to Afghanistan. The minister told the House of Commons that a one-thousand-member battle group and brigade level headquarters would operate in the Kabul area as part of the UN-mandated ISAF mission. "Canada is willing to serve with a battle group and brigade headquarters for a period of one year starting late this summer," McCallum explained.[7]

From August 2003 to the summer of 2005, the Canadian mission was mainly limited to Operation Athena, the ISAF effort in Kabul to stabilize the government there. In February 2005, however, NATO defence ministers, including Canada's Bill Graham, had met in Brussels and planned for the extension of the alliance's operations across Afghanistan to commence in early 2006. Following the meeting, Graham told reporters that Canada "would be opening a new PRT [Provincial Reconstruction Team]" to begin in the summer of 2005.[8] Underlying the concept of the PRTs was the idea that NATO countries should undertake responsibility for operations in designated regions of Afghanistan. As well as providing security and, if necessary, offensive military force against the insurgency, the PRTs were to include civilian personnel who would help train Afghan police and assist in the construction and opening of schools and hospitals and in the rebuilding of infrastructure.

The Canadian PRT was to be located in the Kandahar region in an area of Afghanistan where the Taliban was strongest and where Canadians would be involved in anti-insurgency warfare. The assignment was much different than the security mission that Canadians had been responsible for in Kabul. In late June 2005, an advance guard of two hundred Canadian soldiers headed for Kandahar to set up a base to house the members of the PRT, which would include RCMP officers, members of the Canadian International Development Agency (CIDA), and Foreign Affairs personnel in addition to soldiers.[9] Commandos from the JTF-2 were expected to provide security for the team—an expectation confirmed in an announcement by the Chief of Defence Staff, General Rick Hillier, two weeks later. A few days earlier Hillier had come to the attention of Canadians as a man who would not act like a quiet civil servant in public in the manner of his predecessors when he declared that the purpose of the military was "to be able to kill people" such as the terrorists Canada was fighting in Afghanistan. The general depicted his target "as murderers and scumbags" who "detest" the freedoms enjoyed by the citizens of democratic countries.[10]

By the end of November 2005, with the departure of the last Canadians from Camp Julien in Kabul, the base they had constructed in the spring of 2003, the Canadian mission was focused on the much more dangerous task in Kandahar. In the early months of 2006 Canadian troop strength in the south was ramped up to 2,200 soldiers.

The Canadians began taking over duties that had previously been performed by the U.S. Task Force Gun Devil. At a ceremony to mark the handover of operations to the Canadians, U.S. Lt.-Col. Bert Gees, the head of Task Force Gun Devil, told the Canadians: "When the enemy rears its ugly head, I expect you to kill and capture them and defeat them. Keep up the aggressiveness and continue on the fight against the enemy." He added, "The change today is similar to a line change in hockey. It's still the same team going down the ice ready to score, just a different capability out there."[11]

On February 26, 2006, Canadian Brigadier-General David Fraser assumed command of the multinational operation in southern Afghanistan. He took charge of a force of 8,000 NATO soldiers, including 2,200 Canadians, as well as Afghan units in the region. These forces were deployed where the insurgency was most robust. Fraser would maintain command of southern operations until November 1, 2006, when he relinquished command to Dutch Major-General Ton van Loon.

For the Canadians, this mission proved to be bloody and difficult. The Canadian forces, which had been involved in Operation Mountain Thrust, the largest battle in the war since the invasion of Afghanistan in 2001, moved into the Panjwai area in July 2006,[12] with the support of Afghan units and backed up by U.S., British, and Dutch forces. The purpose of the Canadian offensive—in what would prove to be a multi-phased battle—was to clear a region where the Taliban had enjoyed notable success in entrenching itself and holding onto territory. Days of heavy fighting, during which one Canadian soldier was killed, led to the clearing of the Taliban out of the area and the breaking up of their large formations. After Canadian and Afghan troops left the area, however, the Taliban moved back in, becoming a thorn in the side of the Canadian operations in the Kandahar region. The second phase of the battle commenced in September when the Canadians launched Operation Medusa, whose purpose was to break up Taliban units and deprive the enemy of its hold on the area. While the Canadians quickly gained the strategic upper hand, the price was high. On the second day of the offensive, four Canadians died in two attacks, and on the following day another Canadian soldier was killed and thirty were wounded when a U.S. aircraft accidentally fired on Canadian troops after the Canadians had called for air support. The operation was successful in re-establishing Canadian control of the Panjwai area, but Taliban hit and run attacks continued there nonetheless.

During the first ten months of 2007, Canadian soldiers continued to fight in the area around Kandahar, over terrain that had been secured from the insurgents, then reoccupied by them and taken again by the Canadians. Casualties continued to mount. One tragic incident on June 20, in which three Canadian soldiers were killed forty kilometres west of Kandahar, in the Panjwai District, illustrated how difficult the slogging match had become.[13] The three died when their unarmoured all-terrain vehicle was struck by a bomb blast in what was thought to be a secure area. Insurgents had managed to penetrate the zone to plant the explosives. Increasingly the Taliban's tactics had turned to the use of improvised explosive devices, which made forays by Canadian and other NATO soldiers from their bases more difficult and compelled them to consider the deployment of more heavily armoured vehicles.

The heavier fighting and the rise in Canadian casualties sparked a sharper political debate about the war in Canada. In early October

2006 Prime Minister Harper staked out his position. Speaking in Calgary, where he was receiving the Woodrow Wilson Award for public service, he declared, "The mounting Canadian death toll in Afghanistan is the price of leadership that comes with playing a significant role in global affairs."[14] The same week Hillier, who had just returned from Afghanistan, declared in a television interview that despite the Canadian casualties the morale among the Canadian soldiers in the zone of conflict remained high. "They know they've got great support back here in Canada," Hillier said.[15]

A few weeks before the prime minister's Calgary speech, at its convention in Quebec City, the federal NDP called for Canadian soldiers to be withdrawn from the combat in Afghanistan. Just before the NDP convention, party leader Jack Layton explained the thinking behind his party's position on the war:

> Our efforts in the region are overwhelmingly focussed on military force—spending defence dollars on counter-insurgency. Prime Minister Harper need only look at the experience in Iraq to conclude that ill-conceived and unbalanced missions do not create the conditions for long-term peace. Why are we blindly following the defence policy prescriptions of the Bush administration?
>
> This is not the right mission for Canada. There is no balance— in particular it lacks a comprehensive rebuilding plan and commensurate development assistance....
>
> That's why I'm announcing that as a first step, New Democrats are calling for the withdrawal of Canadian troops from the combat mission in southern Afghanistan. Withdrawal should

begin as soon as possible—working with our international partners to ensure a safe and smooth transition—but with a view to
having it complete by February 2007.[16]

During 2007 Harper twice adjusted his public stance on the
Afghanistan mission. In June he stated that the future of the mission
after February 2009 would depend on what kind of consensus could be
reached in Parliament on the issue. On the strength of this statement, it
appeared that the Conservatives were shying away from their previous
stance, which had been to "stay the course," to continue the military
mission as long as it was needed. Concerned about public opinion that
left the Conservatives mired with the support of about one-third of the
electorate, and worried that gains in Quebec would not materialize
as long as the government stuck to its stand, the prime minister was
changing course. Then came three by-elections in Quebec in September, in which the Conservatives won a rural seat from the Bloc Québé-
cois and the Liberals lost their stronghold in Outremont to the NDP. The
result left new Liberal leader Stéphane Dion wounded and Harper and
his strategists looking for ways of triggering an early election. Buoyed
by his brighter electoral prospects, the prime minister tacked again on
the issue of Afghanistan, saying that what he sought was a parliamentary majority on the issue. His hopes that he would soon lead a majority
government meant that he now expected to be able to set the course in
Afghanistan himself. He was thus veering back to his preferred option—
continuing the military mission until victory was achieved.

How long might the war in Afghanistan go on? On that subject
the Canadian military and members of the Conservative government

had little to say. Others have not been so circumspect. In October 2007, in an interview with the *Sunday Telegraph*, the British commander in Afghanistan's Helmand province made a frank estimate of the possibilities. "This is a counter-insurgency operation which is going to take time," he explained. "It could last a decade. The counter-narcotic problem, which is huge, could take another 25 years. The British ambassador has said it will take 30 years. He has often said that this mission is a marathon, not a sprint, and he is absolutely right."[17]

Given political developments in the United States, Pakistan, and Afghanistan itself, there are cogent reasons for believing that the war will not last nearly so long, at least in its present form. Nevertheless, with heavy combat for Canadian units underway and with the political parties staking out their ground on the issue, Canadians had to consider what they thought of this war in a way that they had not had to think about any war since the Korean conflict.

The basic questions remained to be addressed. What were we doing in this bloody conflict on the other side of the world? What interests did we have in the fight? Canadians also learned, in news reports, to their discontent, that the Taliban insurgents our forces were fighting could slip out of harm's way across the border into Pakistan, where they could find a safe haven until they returned to hit us again. Canadians were discovering that this war had a dirty underside, that good and evil were not so simply arrayed against each other as they had been told.

By February 2008, seventy-eight Canadian soldiers and one Canadian diplomat had been killed in Afghanistan. From autumn 2001 to spring 2006, Canada's military mission in Afghanistan cost more than $4.1 billion. Prior to 2001 Canada's relationship with Afghanistan had been minor, with Canadian aid to the country averaging about $10 million a year. Since then Afghanistan has become the largest single recipient of Canadian bilateral aid in the world. At an international conference in Tokyo in January 2002, Canada pledged a dramatic increase in its aid to Afghanistan. According to the Department of Foreign Affairs and International Development (DFAIT), Canada had committed $616.5 million to the war-torn country covering the period 2001 to 2009.[18] The $4.1 billion spent on Canadian military operations in Afghanistan by the spring of 2006 dwarfs the amount allocated by Canada as aid to Afghanistan.[19] In practice the ratio of military to non-military spending by Canada in Afghanistan is more than ten to one.

Canadians have long proudly thought of their nation as a major participant in UN peacekeeping missions. To put Canada's Afghanistan mission into perspective, let us consider the resources devoted to it as compared with Canadian peacekeeping efforts. While Canada has well over two thousand military personnel stationed in Afghanistan, this country now deploys only fifty-nine military personnel to UN missions worldwide. There are now over sixty-four thousand military personnel posted with UN missions around the globe, and they are drawn from ninety-five countries. Canada's contribution to these missions, in terms of personnel, amounts to a mere 0.09 per cent. This places us fiftieth out of ninety-five in our contribution of military personnel to UN missions. Prior to the mid-1990s, Canada consistently ranked among the top ten countries in its contributions of personnel to UN military operations.[20]

■ ■

4

To Support the Troops, Take Cover Behind Them

CANADA'S HISTORY HAS BEEN DRAMATICALLY MARKED and altered by war. The two world wars, during which one hundred thousand Canadian soldiers perished, played a crucial role in transforming the country from a British dominion to an industrialized nation. The mobilization of military forces—some six hundred thousand strong in World War I and a million strong in World War II—strained the very fabric of Confederation, pitting English and French Canadians against each other in searing battles over conscription. When Canada emerged from the Second World War, it was one of the world's leading industrial and military powers. The stamp of the military on daily Canadian life was enormous. Thousands of demobilized soldiers entered universities and permanently changed the character of those institutions. Many of the male teachers in primary and especially secondary schools in Canada were veterans of one of the world wars.

At Oakwood Collegiate in Toronto, where I attended my first years of high school in the 1950s, we addressed our male teachers according to their military rank—captain, lieutenant, colonel, or major. Remembrance Day, November 11, was a huge occasion, devoted to reminding us of the impact of the wars on Canada. Our principal, a veteran of the First World War, broke down in tears at the school assembly as he told us of his lost comrades in arms. Each spring the boys in the school, having trained all year with rifles and in uniform, participated in a military inspection at the Fort York Armoury, where we were inspected by a high-ranking military officer. These were the days of the Korean conflict, and we were well aware of Canada's participation in the war.

After Korea, despite Canada's continuing membership in NATO and later in the North American Aerospace Defence Command (NORAD), Canadian society evolved in a way that would have been unimaginable in the first half of the twentieth century. Canada did not directly participate in the Vietnam War, and that experience—of not participating—changed the country, just as participation in the world wars and Korea had transformed it in earlier decades. Beginning in the late 1950s and in subsequent decades, the Canadian Forces were involved in peacekeeping operations in many parts of the world.

As the great wars receded into history and Canada sent troops to serve in peacekeeping missions, the Canadian identity, with respect to matters military, shifted dramatically. Unlike our major allies, such as the United States, United Kingdom, France, West Germany, and Italy, Canada had no compulsory military service for young men following the Second World War. After the 1950s, most young men and women in Canada had no direct contact with the military. While millions of Canadians had ancestors who had served in the military—my father went overseas as an artillery officer in the Second World War—except for certain regions of the country, such as the Maritimes, where military service was more common, younger Canadians had little knowledge of the Canadian Forces.

In the decades following the Second World War a new outlook evolved in Canada, an outlook placing a premium on efforts to achieve peace. The outlook is anti-militarist, or at least non-militarist, albeit with important regional differences. Quebec, with its history of struggles against conscription during the two world wars, is much more anti-militarist than Alberta is. Other provinces and regions tend to lie between these two poles in their outlook.

Canada participated in the first Gulf War and the war in Kosovo during the 1990s. In both wars, the Canadian Forces did not suffer any casualties. Afghanistan has been different. The many deaths of our soldiers—the first significant losses for the Canadian military since Korea—have been a searing experience. With this war, and the evident lack of desire of so much of the country to participate in it, has come a concerted campaign to promote militarism. Although the focus has been Afghanistan, the goals of the campaign extend far beyond the current mission. The Harper government, and more broadly the active political right, along with much of the Canadian media, various intellectuals, writers, and personalities, spokespersons for the Canadian Forces, and pro-military lobbyists, are united in a drive to win the support of Canadians for a much more muscular military. On their agenda is the idea that Canada should build a military machine and use it where it matters, on the battlefield. Peacekeeping, in the eyes of the pro-militarists, is for Europeans and other weak-kneed people.

While the pro-militarist campaign has been taken up by many people and institutions on their own initiative, it has also seen a great deal of co-ordination. The Conservative government has played a crucial role and has not hesitated to provide muscle for this political effort, which has nothing do with the legitimate functions of the Department of National Defence or of other government departments.

The heightened attention of the Canadian Forces to the battle for public opinion was highlighted in June 2007 on the eve of the departure of the Quebec-based Van Doos (Royal 22nd Regiment) to Afghanistan. For both the government and the military, Quebec was a particular concern because of the low level of support in the province for the mission in Afghanistan. A poll by Leger Marketing showed that 70 per cent of Quebeckers opposed sending the Van Doos to Afghanistan.[1] In advance of the regiment's departure, Quebec-based soldiers visited a dozen cities in Quebec to present them with their regimental flag so the communities could fly it for the duration of the team's deployment in Afghanistan. For its part, the military would fly the flags of the municipalities at its base in Kandahar.

The main event in showcasing the Van Doos to Quebeckers and other Canadians was a military parade, starring the regiment, through the streets of the provincial capital. The day before the parade, two thousand soldiers from the regiment held a tailgate party in Montreal and then watched the Alouettes play the Toronto Argonauts.

In Quebec City, military spokespersons urged the public to support the troops whether or not they favoured the mission in Afghanistan. That tactic—attempting to rally support for the soldiers even among those who oppose the mission—has been used right across the country. Explaining the approach of the military in Quebec to a reporter for *The Toronto Star*, spokesperson Lt.-Cmdr. Hubert Genest said: "We're trying to make a public event . . . so that we can engage the public and try to explain once again what the mission is all about. It's a challenge. . . . We feel that we have a part to play in trying to inform the public about what we're trying to achieve."

Genest added: "If those groups who are criticizing the mission have a right to express their view in the protest, we exercise our right in what we think in parading and saying goodbye to our loved ones."[2]

The quotes are revealing. In his remarks the military spokesperson does not limit himself to saying only that the military has a right to say "goodbye to our loved ones," but also asserts that they have a role in "trying to inform the public about what we're trying to achieve." The hope here is that loyalty to the troops, or at least reticence about criticizing them, will silence critics who disagree with the mission.

Naturally enough, those who have publicly demonstrated in opposition to Canada's mission in Afghanistan do not want to be perceived as being hostile to the soldiers who wear the nation's uniform. When the Van Doos paraded through Quebec City, they were met by well-wishers, but also by protesters, who went out of their way to explain that they were there to criticize the mission but not the troops. As Mathilde Forest-Rivière explained to a CTV news reporter, "We want to tell people that we are against sending our troops to Afghanistan, because this war is unjustified."[3]

Also in June 2007, around the same time as the military was attempting to foster sympathy among Quebeckers, the question of whether support for the troops means support for the mission triggered a loud debate in Toronto City Council. The issue was what to do about "Support Our Troops" decals on official city vehicles, including fire engines and ambulances. The decals, which had been on the vehicles for a period of months, were originally scheduled to be removed in September. Those who wanted the decals to remain in place used the issue to paint those who wanted them removed as being disloyal to Canada's soldiers.

Initially Mayor David Miller said it was "appropriate" to remove the decals as planned, observing that to many people they symbolized a "very controversial military operation." The mayor and city councillors who backed his position changed their minds when they found themselves up against a furious reaction across the country, channelled through call-in radio shows. In Toronto the campaign was spearheaded by city councillor Frances Nunziata, who brought a motion before the council to extend the decals campaign for as long as Canada was at war in Afghanistan.

A popular interactive Internet news site received a number of comments on the issue: "A fine way to show loyalty to the men and women fighting, or getting wounded, or worst of all, going home in flag draped coffins," wrote one enraged citizen. "All we want to do is repay the loyalty with a bit of gratitude. I guess that is out of bounds for the meddlesome councilors of Toronto City Council.... They have added more fuel to the fire as to why Toronto is hated outside of the GTA." Talk of boycotting Toronto during the upcoming summer holidays was aired. "If Toronto doesn't want to support our troops, then I don't think I can support Toronto with my vacation money. Scratch my visit to Toronto. Boycott Toronto everyone," wrote one man.[4]

As the city council debate reached its climax, three more Canadian soldiers were killed in Afghanistan. Mayor Miller introduced a motion to continue the decal campaign with the proviso that the "Support Our Troops" campaign refer to "all Canadian troops" and not to the duration of the mission in Afghanistan. The mayor explained to the media that the "deaths of the three members of the military" had caused him to change his mind. Miller's motion was adopted by a vote of 39-0, with a number of councillors absenting themselves because they couldn't support it.[5]

Among those who did not vote was Councillor Pam McConnell. "My father died (in World War II) and so I was orphaned by the war," she explained. "My nephew has returned (from Afghanistan) and I am aware this is a war.... In order to show my support for both my father, my nephew and other people who are being hurt, maimed and who have died in wars, I left the chamber. I felt it was the most important thing I could do. I was not going to vote against my conscience or my beliefs." McConnell observed that though she supported the troops— "How can you not support people who are giving their lives?"—she also believed in the importance of making a statement against the war in Afghanistan.

Also absent was Councillor Janet Davis, who explained that she didn't believe city vehicles should be used to "promote political messages." Although she supported the troops, she did not favour extending the decal campaign.

In Calgary, in the heartland of the province where support for the Afghanistan mission was highest, a contentious debate took place in July 2007 about whether to put "Support Our Troops" decals on city vehicles. In the end the municipal government decided not to apply the decals. Instead, council unanimously approved Mayor Dave Bronconnier's plan to sell decals to the public to raise money for military families. Alberta premier Ed Stelmach announced that the provincial government would not make it mandatory to put decals on city vehicles, but that decals would be made available to civic employees, who could then decide for themselves whether to affix them or not.[6]

An initiative in Ontario to rally support for the troops, and through them for the war, came in the form of a petition calling on the Ontario government to rename a portion of Canada's busiest highway. The idea was to honour the Canadian soldiers killed in Afghanistan by designating the 172-kilometre-long section of Highway 401 from Trenton to Toronto as the "Highway of Heroes," thus commemorating their sacrifice. That particular roadway was chosen because when soldiers who die in Afghanistan are repatriated to Canada, their bodies are first flown to the Canadian Forces Base at Trenton and then the remains are driven along the highway to Toronto, where autopsies are performed. Groups of people in the communities along the 401 have made a practice of gathering on overpasses to salute the fallen soldiers as the hearses bearing their remains pass below.

The petition was originally launched by James Forbes, a twenty-two-year-old resident of London, Ontario, who planned to enlist in the armed forces. It garnered the support of fourteen thousand signatories online. In mid-August 2007, with a provincial election two months away, the Ontario government embraced the idea of renaming the stretch of highway. The province's transportation minister, Donna Cansfield, told Canadian Press: "I think when you consider the sacrifice that the soldiers and others have made, it's just a wonderful opportunity for us to reflect on that sacrifice and to be able to acknowledge it."

After the centennial of Confederation in 1967, Highway 401 was renamed as the Macdonald-Cartier Freeway in honour of two leading Fathers of Confederation. In fact, there is already a highway honouring the military in Ontario: Highway 416, which connects Ottawa to the 401, has been designated "Veterans Memorial Highway."

The campaign in support of the Highway of Heroes petition was mounted and run by members of Milnet.ca, a website promoting a pro-military outlook.

Far from being a grassroots outpouring of the sentiments of ordinary Canadians, the campaign for the Highway of Heroes was masterminded and managed by a small, highly right-wing, pro-military pressure group—not at all representative of Ontario society— whose purpose was to raise the profile and acceptance of the military in Canada. These people have an unassailable right to organize and to proselytize. But their role in the petition was not covered by the media, as it should have been. Some fourteen thousand signatures is not a large number, as these things go. Many other causes could easily muster this number of supporters, indeed many more, without stampeding a provincial government into renaming a highway. With uncharacteristic haste, the Ontario Ministry of Transportation had the Highway of Heroes signs mounted along Highway 401 by the autumn of 2007.

Initiatives to rally support for the troops and to win Canadians over to the idea that the Canadian Forces are fundamental to the Canadian identity—and that the power of the nation is measured by their strength and effectiveness—have come in a variety of packages. In

On its "About This Site" page, the founder and owner of the Milnet.ca website describes its purpose:

General

This website was created to provide information about the Canadian Army to:

- past and present members of the military
- potential recruits
- military and civilian organizations
- anyone with an interest in Canada's Army

Background

Army.ca first came online in December of 1993, under the name of The Canadian Army Home Page. At the time, it was Canada's first military site on the Internet. Since that time, the page has grown considerably, and is always in some stage of development. Much of the information has come from visitors to the page, who have graciously taken the time to contribute information, making a much better site.

Army.ca currently consists of thousands of pages containing of a wide variety of information and from a number of sources.

Administration

Army.ca is owned and maintained [by] Mike Bobbitt, with the generous help of many Staff, senior members and subscribers.

Army.ca is maintained primarily through subscriptions and advertising, and sometimes from Mike's personal funds.

Disclaimer

Army.ca is a private effort, and is in no way sponsored by or connected to the Department of National Defence, the Canadian Forces, or any other military organization. Army.ca is not supported in any manner, either official or unofficial. As a result, it often does not get the time or resources that it often requires, however it also means that it can operate without the worry of following official administrative guidelines and restrictions.

Despite this freedom, Army.ca attempts to provide accurate and timely information of interest to serving and potential members of the CF, however any information obtained from this page comes "as is" and it's [sic] accuracy cannot be guaranteed.

June 2007 Ottawa decided that the appropriate way to commemorate Canada's contribution to the achievement of peace in Northern Ireland was to send a warship to Belfast. *The Globe and Mail* headlined the story: "Warship's arrival signals Canada's new international muscle."

Considering that the role Canada played in the peace process in Northern Ireland was a stellar example of the efficacy of "soft power," it is striking that the government chose a warship, the symbol of hard power, to mark the occasion.

Using the airwaves as the medium to express his unflinching support for things military has been Don Cherry, the star of "Coach's Corner" on *Hockey Night in Canada*. Cherry has frequently abandoned hockey to turn his broadcast into a bully pulpit on behalf of the military. In 2003 Cherry appeared on the segment wearing an American-flag-pattern tie. He scolded the Canadian government for not supporting the U.S. military effort in Iraq. In the summer of 2007 the Royal Canadian Legion saluted Cherry by making him an honorary life member. Interviewed about the award, Cherry said: "What gets me is whether you feel the mission is right or wrong, to put it down only puts our troops down. If you don't support the mission, that only encourages the enemy and makes it want to turn it on all the more."[7]

Cherry said what those in the decal fight in Toronto had implied— to support the troops, you had to support the mission in Afghanistan.

The tactic of insisting that to support the troops citizens had to endorse the mission had a pernicious logic. It was the Government of Canada that decided on the mission and sent the troops into combat. The men and women who enlisted in the Canadian Forces had nothing to do with determining the nature, scope, and duration of the mission. Indeed, the soldiers are among the least politically influential citizens in Canada. It is the grave responsibility of a country's political leadership and citizenry to decide when to send young men and women into harm's way. Once the government has made its choice, it is nothing less than cowardly to turn reality on its head and to insist that the only way to support the troops is to stand blindly behind a mission that the soldiers played no role in choosing. In the precarious political situation in which the minority Harper government found itself, the Conservatives and their supporters selected this tactic— they hide behind the soldiers in the field and demand that everyone else do the same thing.

■ ■

The cat and mouse game about whether citizens were being asked to support the troops or the mission was one that virtually all the major supporters of the deployment in Afghanistan were playing. On Friday, August 24, 2007, Defence Minister Peter MacKay, General Rick Hillier, Don Cherry, and Toronto Police Chief Bill Blair were speakers at a rally at the Canadian National Exhibition to support the troops. The event, dubbed "Red Friday"—those in attendance were asked to wear red to display their support—was billed as demonstrating support for the troops, and ended up as a rally on behalf of the mission in Afghanistan and its goals.

"The rally today means so much to our troops, it means so much to the men and women who are working hard to protect us, to safeguard our freedoms and the lives of the people in Afghanistan and to those who want to live in an open and free country like ours," MacKay told the crowd of about one thousand. "Being here today shows that we greatly, deeply appreciate their work. Being here means that you recognize the tremendous sacrifices that go along with this mission."

General Hillier assured the crowd that the troops in Afghanistan would see pictures of the rally and appreciate the support. "What that does is convince them that when they're 12,000 kilometres away from home and when you're on a dusty, dirty and dangerous trail, and when you're walking that trail doing your mission, Canadians are walking with them."[8]

At events such as this, government ministers and top members of the military were hiding behind the troops to garner support for a mission that half the country did not back. Their goal was to cow the opponents of the mission into silence. Only time would tell whether this tactic would bear fruit politically. Another possible outcome, perhaps more likely, was that pressuring Canadians into supporting a mission about which they had grave doubts would foster resistance, anger, and a good deal of cynicism about flag-waving and flashy patriotism.

A major problem for those pushing the pro-military agenda is that the attitude of Canadians to Afghanistan was influenced by events and debates that were beyond their control. Developments in the Afghanistan conflict, including moves there to negotiate with elements of the Taliban and the role of Pakistan in the war, influenced Canadian attitudes to the conflict. Well beyond the control of the pro-military side in Canada has been the rapid evolution of the debate about the wars in Iraq and Afghanistan in the United States.

Not content to allow the debate about the role of the military and the Afghanistan mission to take shape in the media and among political parties, the federal government has weighed in to the effort to shape opinion through initiatives undertaken by government departments and agencies.

To see how directly the Department of National Defence participates in the effort to enlist support for the Afghanistan mission, I decided to visit the department website, where I found a menu item that suggested "Support Our Troops." Clicking on that, and then on another item, "Buy Support Our Troops merchandise," I emerged in a cornucopia of products that anyone can purchase to show support. For sale, as "official" merchandise sanctioned by the Canadian Forces, is a long list of baseball caps, T-shirts, car and refrigerator magnets, cling vinyl window decals, lapel pins, and other items. The proceeds from the sale of these items are used to fund "morale and welfare programs" for Canadian soldiers and their families.

The list of Support Our Troops paraphernalia runs on for many pages. An assortment of ball caps in varying colours and designs can be had for $14.99. Banner flags and car flags go for $19.99 and $12.99 respectively. Boys' and girls' shirts are available in French or English. There is a long line of T-shirts for women and girls emblazoned with "Ladies Air Force" (or army or navy) and "Girls Rule." Boys' and men's clothing follows, along with a "Support Our Troops" dog tag with chain or bracelet. At the top of the list of items is a CD, *The Red and White*, with songs and lyrics by country singer Julian Austin, who has performed at frequent tours for Canadian troops. The chorus of his signature song, "The Red and White," proclaims:

This country sometimes,

Makes me so damn mad I could cry

. Cause we never thank our heroes enough anymore.[9]

On the "Support Our Troops" page Canadians are urged to "wear something red on Fridays to show support for the Canadian Forces and their families."

Such appeals did not win universal acclaim. Writing in the *Ottawa Citizen*, Janice Kennedy explained why she wouldn't wear red.

> Last fall, I had the privilege of spending time with several women in Petawawa, military wives who had soldier husbands serving in Afghanistan.... They impressed the heck out of me. Still do, when I think of them. Because of women like them—and the obviously good men overseas they worried about constantly and spoke of so lovingly—I was happy to make the simple, undemanding gesture of wearing red for a few Fridays. But I felt compelled to stop some time ago. What used to be an uncomplicated show of pure human support has become political, and the politics is distinctly ugly. Under Canada's New Government, we're witnessing the rise of Canada's New Militarism.[10]

■ ■

In September 2007 I filed a request under the *Access to Information Act* for records from the Department of Foreign Affairs and International Trade in relation to the federal government's "communications plans, strategic public affairs plans, media relations plans, plans for promotional activity, plans for community outreach," etc., having to do with Canada's mission in Afghanistan. The request covered the period August 15, 2007 to October 15, 2007. As it turned out I cut back drastically on the range of dates, and the scope of documents sought, after being informed that my original request would take many months to be filled. On January 10, 2008, I finally received a set of documents from the department, subject to a few redactions. (My request for documents from three other departments and agencies had not been met by that date.)

The documents from DFAIT made abundantly clear what the Harper government wanted Canadians to think about the mission in Afghanistan and exposed its strategy for managing the public relations campaign. Planners, for instance, proposed a "message event" to be held on September 4, 2007, in the National Press Theatre in Ottawa to update journalists on "recent events and achievements in Afghanistan." The briefings were described as "technical" and were to be held every six weeks.

Participants at the briefing were to be David Mulroney, associate deputy minister of DFAIT; Stephen Wallace, vice-president of the Policy Branch of CIDA; a senior official from the Department of National Defence; and a spokesperson from the RCMP who was to be present but not officially briefing. The only person to speak on the record for attribution was to be the Canadian ambassador to Afghanistan, Arif Lalani, participating via teleconference from Afghanistan. The other briefers could be quoted, but their remarks were to be "attributed only to a 'senior government official.'" On the business day prior to September 4, there was to be a "dry run" of the briefing.

The target audience for the briefing was the Ottawa-based media as well as regional media via teleconference. The document spelled out the "desired soundbite" to come out of the briefing: "Canada is assisting Afghanistan to help alleviate poverty, restore the rule of law and create a secure and stable environment for the Afghan people."

A number of "key messages" were to be transmitted via the media to Canadians:

- We are making steady progress on the ground.
- Helping Afghanistan continues the noble Canadian tradition of taking an active role in bringing stability and peace to parts of the world that have seen turmoil and upheaval.
- Afghanistan is Canada's largest recipient of bilateral development assistance and we are among the top donors in the world with over $100 million in annual development assistance and a total pledge of $1.2 billion until 2011.
- Canada has shown leadership by committing development assistance and deploying diplomats, development workers, troops and civilian police to help the Afghan government secure a better future for its people.
- We are making progress—unthinkable only a few years ago—which is a testament to the will and fortitude of the Afghan people, as well as to the commitment and engagement of the international community.

- Military forces from 37 countries, including Canada,
  are involved in the UN-sanctioned, NATO-led mission
  at the request of the Afghan Government. Over 60
  countries and numerous international organizations
  are supporting the Afghanistan Compact—a frame-
  work for cooperation between the Afghanistan government and the international community over the
  next five years—and its objectives. There are also over
  20 UN agencies on the ground.

The documents show that over the following weeks other events
and briefings were held with very much the same "desired soundbite"
and "key messages" as the objectives. These happenings involved Foreign Affairs Minister Maxime Bernier, Michel de Salaberry, senior civilian co-ordinator of the Provincial Reconstruction Team in Kandahar,
Canadian diplomats, and others, and included journalists from different regions of the country. For instance, a group of six journalists
from Trois-Rivières, Chicoutimi, Winnipeg, Owen Sound, Victoria, and
Regina, who were travelling to Afghanistan (their names were redacted
in the document), were briefed at the Trenton air force base prior to
their departure. One of the stated "strategic objectives" of the briefing
was "to highlight how Canadian efforts are contributing to reconstruction, development and capacity building in Afghanistan and encour-
aging the spread of freedom, democracy, the rule of law and respect
for human rights."

One document showed that the government was well aware
that young Canadians were less than enthusiastic about the country's

Afghanistan mission. As "Canada in Afghanistan: Connecting with Young Canadians" explained, "The Afghanistan Task Force is promoting youth outreach activities with the aim of creating dialogue and building partnerships among Canadian youth." The document frankly acknowledged the need for dialogue: "In relation to Canada's foreign policy priority of rebuilding Afghanistan, young Canadians are the most skeptical and passive demographic."

The same essential messages were drummed home repeatedly with all the target audiences, and never varied depending on what was actually happening in Afghanistan. The effort was to manage public opinion, rather than to critically inform Canadians about the prospects for the mission. The Harper government was determined to control communications on Afghanistan and to paint a rosy picture of events there. Under its direction DFAIT had been reduced to a wartime propaganda agency.

The Harper government and its media, intellectual, and other allies have set out to reconfigure the Canadian identity, placing the "manly" attributes of militarism at the centre. The Support Our Troops campaign, the Highway of Heroes petition, the use of personalities such as Don Cherry, and the high-profile role of General Rick Hillier to promote the military have all been aspects of the effort to change the culture.

To put it more precisely, the goal is to make existing elements of Canadian culture more prominent. The appeal is to a supposedly manly ethic that revels in a brutal brand of hockey, in which force trumps skill. Both Cherry and Hillier are masters of bluff male banter, a style of discourse that relies on bullying quips to gratify and cow its listeners. The central narrative in this faux-male culture is that once you find yourself in a fight you see it through to the end. You never question what got you into the brawl in the first place. In this subculture, questioning the reasons for a fight is tantamount to letting down the side.

In spring 2007 the blunt-spoken General Hillier told reporters in Kandahar that Canadian soldiers were mighty disgruntled that their mission in Afghanistan had been eclipsed by allegations that prisoners handed over to the Afghans by Canadians were tortured. Declared the general: "Let me just come out and say very frankly here that I've met a variety of soldiers who are pissed off."[11]

■ ■

5

The Many Invasions of Afghanistan

AFGHANISTAN, A COUNTRY WHOSE POPULATION IS ESTI-
mated at about 31.5 million, has been invaded many times over the
millennia. In his whirlwind conquests in the fourth century B.C., Alexander the Great seized the lands bordering on the Aegean Sea and the
whole of the Persian Empire, driving into Afghanistan and a corner
of India before turning back to the west and occupying Egypt in 332
B.C. During his brief stay on Afghan soil, Alexander left one important legacy, the city of Kandahar, which was named after him. Despite
the forbidding terrain in the heart of Central Asia, Afghan mountain
passes have served as gateways for important commercial routes; and
the Afghan territory as a whole has long been prized for its strategic
value in imperial struggles.

The Russians and the British invaded the country on a number of
occasions, ultimately concluding that local resistance made Afghanistan too much trouble to be worth long-term occupation. During
the nineteenth century the British and the Russians eyed each other's

empires across the territory of Afghanistan in what came to be known as "the great game." The British feared that if the Russians gained control of Afghanistan, they could push through the Khyber Pass and threaten British India. The Khyber Pass has been the legendary route for invasions going in both directions over thousands of years. It was the route that Alexander the Great took as he left Afghan territory for his foray into India. The British forces in India were woefully under-manned should a Russian force descend on them. The British had always relied on the power of the Royal Navy to sustain their Indian empire. A threat from a great land-based power to the north would pose a much different kind of challenge.

For those who analyzed the geo-politics of the late nineteenth century, the favourite war they imagined was that between Russia and Britain, a war that would have had Afghanistan as its strategic cen-tre. Among others, Karl Marx thought it likely that this terrain would provide the site of the next great war to break out among the imperial powers. That war was never fought, but its absence did not stop both the Russians and the British from maintaining a continuing interest in Afghanistan.

To counter the Russian threat and to gain a predominant role in this strategically vital territory, the British fought three wars, known as the Anglo-Afghan wars, that spanned two centuries.[1] Early on Brit-ish military planners in Calcutta concluded that the safety of India required a *cordon sanitaire*, a swath of territory, including Afghanistan, which would be safely under British sway. The first Anglo-Afghan War, 1839–42, an effort to reduce Afghanistan to a dependency, resulted in a humiliating defeat. The British garrison in Kabul was expelled, and during a wretched winter retreat to the Khyber Pass the British forces were very nearly decimated. The war helped to develop the reputation of the Afghans in the English-speaking world as ferocious fighters in their resistance to foreign occupation of their country. To restore their prestige, tarnished by the disaster, the British launched raids deep into Afghanistan, where they put villages, crops, and livestock to the torch.

The second Anglo-Afghan War, 1878–80, was waged when the existing Afghan regime refused to concede a favoured position to the British in Kabul. The war ended with regime change in Afghanistan and resulted in a period of British control over Afghan foreign policy. During this war, Liberal leader William Ewart Gladstone went on a speaking tour of Scotland to denounce the imperialism of the governing Tories. Among other things he charged that in Afghanistan the British had razed villages, leaving their inhabitants destitute and starving.

Late in the nineteenth century the British and Russians agreed on the boundaries for Afghanistan that endure today. During the First World War, Afghanistan remained neutral despite German efforts—playing on some local sympathy—to install a pro-German regime. During the third Anglo-Afghan War, in 1919, the government in Kabul sought to end British control over the country's foreign policy. British intelligence concluded that the Afghans were seeking aid in the form of aircraft and pilots from the newly created Soviet Union. The British, who had had enough of war by then, signed the Treaty of Rawalpindi on August 19, 1919. With the treaty London gave up its decades-old effort to control Afghan foreign policy. August 19 is celebrated by Afghans as their national independence day.

The retreat of the British from Afghanistan did not end the country's miseries at the hands of foreigners. In 1979 the Soviet Union invaded Afghanistan, an intervention that ended in colossal failure. Many date the beginning of the end of the Soviet Union and its Eastern European empire from that abortive adventure.

The Soviet interest in Afghanistan had existed for many decades prior to the invasion. In the 1950s, following a policy that they conceived as part of their global Cold War struggle against the United States and the capitalist West, the Soviets began providing aid to Afghanistan. They built roads, constructed a number of oil pipelines, and established irrigation systems. During the 1970s, local Afghan communists overthrew the Afghan monarchy and established their own regime. Among their leaders was Babrak Karmal, an acclaimed actor and Marxist who was one of the twenty-eight founding members of the People's Democratic Party of Afghanistan (PDPA) in 1965. He was elected to Afghanistan's National Assembly the same year and would serve in that body until 1973. In 1967 the PDPA split into two factions, with Karmal heading a moderate faction that had more contacts with the outside world. In 1978, with the factions now reunited, the party seized control of Afghanistan, with Karmal serving as the regime's deputy premier—though the resumption of factionalism and the rise of his political opponents soon resulted in his demotion to the position of ambassador to Czechoslovakia.

The communist regime promoted land reform, on behalf of the peasantry, and women's equality. The idea of equal rights for women was deeply offensive to conservative elements in the country. The version of Islam practised in rural Afghanistan insisted on the dominance of men and on the required covering of women when they appeared outside their homes. As a result, the PDPA's efforts to modernize Afghanistan met with stubborn resistance. As the country sank into chaos, the Soviets invaded, sending more than one hundred thousand soldiers into the country.[2]

Just as the United States did in its 2001 assault, the Soviet forces quickly secured Kabul and appeared to have overwhelmed their foes. Soviet commandos killed the country's leader, Hafizullah Amin, and after turning out the previous government the Soviets installed Karmal as the country's new head of government. Karmal promised democratic and constitutional reforms. He pledged an end to the death penalty in Afghanistan, the establishment of individual rights and freedoms, and the election of national and local assemblies. But his regime faced fierce and growing opposition in the countryside from guerrilla forces—the Mujahideen.

What is noteworthy is the extent to which the broad division of forces in the war between the Soviets and their client regime versus the Mujahideen in the 1980s is similar to the division of forces in the struggle between the NATO forces and their Afghan allies versus the Taliban in the new century. The Soviets had a firm grip on Kabul and other cities and, also like NATO, promised reform to the people of Afghanistan, including equal rights for women.

Despite the liberal-sounding promises that were made, the Soviets and their Afghan underlings used force to pummel the insurgents into oblivion. The Soviets bombed the rural areas of Afghanistan, destroying villages, farm land, and irrigation systems. This scorched-earth policy killed an enormous number of people, rendered millions

homeless, and pushed the people in large parts of the country into star-
vation. On top of all this carnage, the Soviets sowed the Afghan landscape with tens of thousand of land mines. Over the years the weapons
killed and maimed thousands of people, and they continue today to
take a heavy toll. The ruthlessness of the Soviets and their clients was
reminiscent of the worst atrocities of the Stalinist regime during the
forced industrialization and collectivization of land in the 1930s, when
millions of people died, especially in the Ukraine.

The Jimmy Carter administration in Washington vehemently
opposed the Soviet invasion of Afghanistan, among other things
organizing a boycott by Western countries of the Moscow Olympics in
the summer of 1980. That the Soviets and their clients, although far
from being democrats, were decidedly more pro-women's rights than
were the insurgents did nothing to deter the Carter administration
from supporting the insurgents. From the beginning the Americans
helped organize and fund the armed opposition to the Soviet client
regime. The war that ensued between the Karmal government and the
Mujahideen was both a genuine civil conflict and a proxy Cold War
struggle between the Soviet Union and United States. The war, which
devastated the country, forced several million Afghans to flee their
homeland into the neighbouring regions of Iran and Pakistan. From
sanctuaries outside Afghanistan, these displaced people served as a
recruitment base for the guerrilla forces that fought the Soviet-backed
government. The insurgents were generously financed by the United
States, Saudi Arabia, and Egypt, as well as by China, allowing them to
purchase weapons on a large scale. As the war progressed, the Mujahideen developed a flexible, decentralized fighting force, with units of

about three hundred men each who were able to hit the Soviets and their Afghan allies and then retreat. After several years of conflict, the insurgents possessed many hundreds of small bases in Afghanistan.

The Mujahideen, drawing on money, weapons, and leadership from multiple sources, were never a unified movement. Their most famous leader, of course, was the Saudi citizen Osama bin Laden, a highly effective organizer and the financier of the insurgency. His efforts drew fighters into the country not only from neighbouring Pakistan and Iran, but from many parts of the Muslim world.

For the Soviet Union, the financial and human costs of the war were staggeringly high. In 1989, after a decade of conflict in which fifteen thousand Soviet soldiers perished, Soviet leader Mikhail Gorbachev concluded that his country, whose Eastern European empire was already showing signs of collapse, had to withdraw from Afghanistan. After the Soviets pulled out, their client regime gradually disintegrated, collapsing altogether in 1992, when the forces of the Mujahideen surrounded Kabul and seized it.

The fall of the Soviet regime in Afghanistan was far from being the end of the country's woes. No sooner had the victorious Mujahideen entered the capital than they fell out with each other to wage war for control of the country. During a time of increasing violence, a perception developed among the Pashtun population in the south that they were not sufficiently represented in the shaky government in Kabul. Out of this turmoil, religious scholars and former Mujahideen fighters established the Taliban, with its main base in Kandahar. By 2000 the Taliban had seized control of almost the whole of the country. By that point, the active opposition to the Taliban was limited to a small corner of the country, the fiefdom of the Northern Alliance, which continued to receive UN recognition as the government of Afghanistan. The Northern Alliance would continue its armed struggle against the Taliban regime until, and after, the time of the U.S. invasion of 2001.

Under the leadership of Mullah Mohammad Omar, the Taliban sought to replace rule by the warlords, who had subjected Afghans to misery, corruption, rape, and bloodshed, with a government intent on imposing a very strict version of Islamic or Sharia law. The Taliban regime quickly became notorious for its implementation of public executions and floggings at soccer stadiums. Men had to wear beards and were beaten if they did not. As soon as the Taliban took control in Kabul, girls were banned from attending school and women were forced out of the workforce, a move that created a shortage of labour in both the educational system and health care. Women, who were forced to wear the burka—a full body costume and head-covering exposing only slits for the eyes—were not allowed to leave their homes without a male relative. Women who disobeyed these regulations could be beaten or even killed. Nail polish was banned, and women flouting this regulation were liable to have the tips of their fingers cut off. Kite-flying and other supposedly frivolous activities were prohibited, as was foreign music and television. Taliban extremism became notorious internationally. In 2001 the Taliban regime's destruction of the two-thousand-year-old Buddhist statues in Bamian, seen by Mullah Omar and his associates as idolatrous, led to global condemnation.[3]

In addition to being criticized for its domestic practices, the Taliban regime was harshly condemned internationally for allowing the poppy and heroin trade to continue. In part in response to international protests, the Taliban cracked down on the poppy trade and claimed in summer 2000 that it had reduced the trade by two-thirds. Just as efforts to stamp out the poppy trade have damaged the standing of the present Afghan government in some regions of the country, where the heroin trade forms the base of the economy, Taliban attempts to do the same also led to political alienation and opposition.

Another feature of the Taliban regime, one that was ultimately to bring it to grief, was its willingness to allow Afghan territory to be used as a refuge and training ground for al Qaeda. Al Qaeda, which means "the base," developed from the Arab volunteers who went to Afghanistan during the 1980s to fight the Soviet occupation. In the early 1990s its central operation was based in Sudan. After 1996 it shifted its headquarters to Afghanistan. Osama bin Laden developed close ties with the Taliban leadership, and the result was the establishment of training camps in Afghanistan. In August 1998, following the bombings of the U.S. embassies in Kenya and Tanzania, President Bill Clinton ordered the U.S. military to launch cruise missile attacks against targets in Sudan and Afghanistan. He named al Qaeda as the organization responsible for the embassy attacks and pinpointed Osama bin Laden as the leader of the organization.

The Taliban's approach to theology and society, it must be said, represents only one of many strains in a wide spectrum of Islamic thought and practice, and, clearly, many Islamic scholars are highly critical of this particular bent. According to some scholars, Taliban ideas combine some of the elements of Wahhabism, a strain of Islamic thought dating back to eighteenth-century Saudi Arabia, with customs of the Pashtun regions of Afghanistan. Significantly, then, the Taliban never managed to eliminate all internal opposition to its rule, and after the U.S. assault on Afghanistan yet another Afghan regime was put together, this one including elements of the Northern Alliance. Once again, Afghanistan was invaded from abroad, this time by the world's only superpower and its allies. Once again an Afghan government was constructed, this time to suit the new invaders.

As in the previous invasions of Afghanistan, the overwhelmingly likely outcome is that the West will tire of its mission and withdraw its forces, leaving the various power groups in Afghanistan to sort out their own future. In the meantime, all that will have been achieved is the deepening misery of the people of this unfortunate country.

■ ■

Canada's Allies

UNLIKE CANADA, MOST NATO MEMBER COUNTRIES ARE not enthusiastic about the Afghan mission.

In October 2007, under NATO command, about 35,500 troops were serving in Afghanistan, about one-third of them American. In principle the alliance's mission there is the key priority for NATO members. In reality, while this is a NATO mission, the major partners engaged in serious combat have been the United States, United Kingdom, and Canada. In October 2006 NATO took command of most of the foreign forces in Afghanistan, including twelve thousand of the U.S. troops. Another eight thousand U.S. soldiers remained under U.S. command and were charged with training the Afghan National Army and hunting for al Qaeda members and Taliban leaders.

The levels of engagement have clearly been uneven, as the statistics show. Given the numbers of troops deployed, and particularly the number of participating soldiers killed, the efforts have varied enormously, with only a few nations assuming the main weight of the

NATO Nations and the Deployment of Personnel, September 2007

United States, 17,000 under NATO-ISAF command and an additional 8,000 under U.S. command, 449 deaths.

United Kingdom, 6,700, with an additional 1,400 to be sent, 82 deaths.

Germany, 3,424, 25 deaths. German forces are deployed in the north — the German mandate does not allow German troops to be used in the south and east in fighting against the Taliban insurgency, except in exceptional circumstances.

Canada, 2,500, 71 deaths.

Italy, 2,161, 10 deaths. The mandate of the Italian parliament does not permit Italian troops to participate in fighting against the insurgency in the south and east except in exceptional circumstances.

Netherlands, 1,665, 11 deaths. Netherlands forces have been deployed in various missions, including some operations in the south.

Poland, 1,200, 1 death.

Turkey, 1,150.

France, 1,100, 12 deaths. French forces are deployed in Kabul; French fighter and refuelling aircraft are based in nearby Tajikistan; a French naval squadron, including the aircraft carrier *Charles de Gaulle*, is based in the Indian Ocean.

Denmark, 420, 6 deaths.

Belgium, 370; its main task is to secure the airport at Kabul.

Czech Republic, 224, 1 death.

Norway, 500, 2 deaths.

Romania, 479, 5 deaths.

Spain, 400, 5 deaths. There were also 18 deaths in a helicopter crash in 2005; and 62 died in a plane crash in Turkey in 2003 en route to Spain.

Hungary, 180.

Greece, 170.

Portugal, 150, 1 death.

Estonia, 130, 2 deaths.

Lithuania, 130.

Bulgaria, 100. Bulgaria plans to send 200 more soldiers.

Latvia, 98.

Slovenia, 60.

Slovakia, 57.

Iceland, 9.

Luxembourg, 9.

Others

In addition to these official NATO forces, small units from so-called Partner Nations, including Albania, Austria, Azerbaijan, Croatia, Finland, Macedonia, Ireland, Sweden, and Switzerland, have supplied small units. The largest contribution among these has come from Sweden, with 350 soldiers, and two deaths.

There are also 870 Australian soldiers, with two deaths; and 122 soldiers from New Zealand.

The Afghan National Army deploys 28,600 troops; there are also 30,200 Afghan policemen.

Source: CNN.com/world, U.S. and Coalition Casualties.

fighting. As of October 8, 2007, 707 coalition deaths had occurred in Afghanistan, ranging, in absolute numbers, from the U.S. high of 449 through the middle level of the United Kingdom (82) and Canada (71) to lows of one or two. (Significantly, 62 Spanish soldiers were killed outside of Afghanistan in a plane crash in Turkey in 2003.) The United States, United Kingdom, and Canada accounted for 85 per cent of all personnel killed; but relative to the size of the populations of the countries participating, Canada has suffered the most casualties.

Other important NATO countries, including Germany, France, and Italy, are much less fully engaged. Because of strong political opposition at home to participation in the Afghan war, and the view of the governments in Berlin, Paris, and Rome that the mission will be long and unrewarding, these NATO countries have mostly kept their forces in the safer regions of the north and have placed restrictions on their forces operating in zones of conflict. Some of their forces are not even permitted to go on patrols at night.

At a NATO summit in Latvia in November 2006, the issue of the disproportionate involvement in combat came to a head. Under pressure from the Americans and British, a few allies—notably, the Netherlands, Romania, Slovenia, and Luxembourg—agreed to ease restrictions on the use of their troops in missions against the insurgents. Far more important, however, were the decisions of France, Germany, Italy, and Spain to permit their forces to be deployed in combat situations only in emergencies. In plain language, these large NATO countries were refusing to shift their positions in any significant way. Explaining the decision, Italian prime minister Romano Prodi told journalists, "This has been our clear position from the beginning." He added:

"That also goes for the French President, the German Chancellor, and the Spanish."

Cynicism has surrounded the Afghanistan mission from the very beginning. The Bush administration launched the invasion of the country for broad geopolitical reasons at a time when the key members of the administration had already made up their minds that the place they really wanted a military showdown was in Iraq. From the British, at least, has come a willingness to speak plainly about the conflict—British officers have warned publicly that the war is not being won—while in the United States the conflict has been so wrapped in ideological bunting that little reality has shone through. Among Canada's other NATO allies in Afghanistan, doubt has been pervasive. The continental European countries have sent forces to Afghanistan, but they also made sure that their casualties remained relatively low. Public opinion would not allow them to do otherwise. The August 2007 Angus Reid survey—the one that showed how sceptical Canadians are about the mission—also included poll results for people in the major European NATO countries. Some 63 per cent of respondents in France deemed the NATO military intervention in Afghanistan a failure, with only 12 per cent calling it a success. In Italy the respective percentages were 66 and 18; in Germany, 69 and 15; and in the United Kingdom, 63 and 16.[1] With the exception of the United Kingdom, these countries entered the conflict under overwhelming pressure from Washington. They are there largely to show that they are loyal members of the Western alliance. When it comes to doing serious fighting against the insurgency, they have not done it, nor will they in the future.

Were Canada to withdraw from the mission, it would not jeopardize our relationship with most other NATO countries, because for most of our allies involvement in Afghanistan has been no more than pro forma.

■ ■

7

Pakistan's Duplicitous Role

WITHOUT THE LARGE-SCALE SUPPORT OF PAKISTAN, IT is exceedingly unlikely that the Taliban would ever have taken power in Afghanistan. Pakistan funded the Taliban, provided its forces with armaments, trained Taliban units, recruited fresh manpower for them, and gave diplomatic aid to the Taliban internationally, among other things supporting the virtual embassies established by the Taliban in key countries.

What is more, assurances to the contrary notwithstanding, there is ample evidence that elements of the Pakistani state, and important tribal groupings in the regions of Pakistan that border on Afghanistan, continue to back the Taliban. There is every reason to believe that the motives for this Pakistani intervention in Afghanistan, which predated the terror attacks of September 11, 2001, remain potent to this day and that they will continue to do so in the future.

Pakistan's involvement in Afghanistan proceeds from long-existing geopolitical interests. Pakistan prefers a weak and divided

Afghanistan as its neighbour, and above all does not want Afghanistan to fall too much under the sway of either the Iranians or the Russians. In addition, Pakistan fears the rise, on both sides of the Pakistan-Afghanistan border, of Pashtun nationalist forces that would be inclined to agitate in favour of a separate state that would threaten Pakistan's hold in its border regions. To deflect the Pashtun energies, Pakistan has supported Islamist forces in the region—forces whose goals are theocratic rather than nationalist. It is a dangerous game that Pakistan has been playing, attempting to extinguish one fire by lighting another.

As long ago as the early 1970s, Pakistan played a role in arming various factions in Afghanistan. The ethnic identity of the peoples who live on the Pakistani side of the frontier is virtually identical to that of the peoples on the Afghan side of the border. As a consequence of their ethnic makeup, these regions of Pakistan are semi-autonomous and officially designated as tribal agencies, administered by an agent appointed by the Pakistan government. This administrative arrangement has lessened the reach of Islamabad, the capital, in the border regions. Owing to this governing system, arising from the close ties between peoples on both sides and to mountainous terrain, the frontier area has been highly porous, with smugglers, refugees, and military units able to slip across while being subjected to little control. During the era of the Soviet occupation about two million Afghan refugees crossed the border into Pakistan. In those days the frontier region of Pakistan was the most important base for the Mujahideen in their hit and run raids against the Soviet regime in Kabul. Today, it is the Americans and their allies, among them the Canadian forces in the Afghan south, who are the victims of similar hit and run raids, launched from

Pakistani territory. In the 1980s, however, the Americans were support-
ive of the raids from Pakistan. The CIA covertly pumped $2.3 billion
into the region, to be used by Pakistan to train as many as eighty thousand Mujahideen fighters for the Afghan struggle.[1]

After the Soviet Union withdrew its forces from Afghanistan in
1989, both active and former Pakistani military officers continued training irregular military units in camps in Afghanistan. During the 1990s,
as the warring factions in Afghanistan fought for supremacy, Pakistan
played a considerable role. As late as the spring of 2001, just months
before the September 11 attacks, Pakistani military vehicles were crossing the border on a daily basis, delivering artillery shells, munitions for
Taliban tanks, and rocket-propelled grenades.

As President Pervez Musharraf's recent, and exceedingly frank,
memoir makes clear, Pakistan was heavily pressured into joining the
U.S. War on Terror in autumn 2001.[2] Some two days after the September 11 terror attacks, U.S. deputy secretary of state Richard Armitage
met in Washington with the Pakistani ambassador to the United States
and the visiting head of Pakistan's military intelligence service. As
Musharraf tells the story, Armitage threatened that unless Pakistan,
one of the few countries that maintained diplomatic relations with the
Taliban regime in Kabul, ruptured its ties with the Taliban and enlisted
in the U.S. War on Terror, the Americans would bomb Pakistan "into
the Stone Age." Armitage disputes the language but does not deny
making the threat.

Musharraf explained that his government considered its options
and concluded that it was not realistic for Pakistan to go to war against
the United States. Facing the prospect of a U.S. aerial attack and an

American alliance with Pakistan's historic enemy, India, Musharraf cleaved to the side of the United States under extreme duress. Explaining his decision, the Pakistani president told the CBS television show *60 Minutes*, "One has to think and take actions in the interests of the nation, and that's what I did."[3] Within a few days of the Armitage threat, Pakistan severed ties with the Taliban and began co-operating with the U.S. efforts to stop al Qaeda and Taliban forces from crossing the frontier into Pakistan. That co-operation won Musharraf and his country the fulsome praise of President Bush. In his frequent speeches on the War on Terror, Bush has prominently listed Pakistan and its leader as among his valued allies.

Collaboration at the top between Islamabad and Washington did not mean that co-operation reached all the way to the operational level on the ground—at least not all the time. Reliable reports have revealed that much of the Taliban leadership is installed in regions of Pakistan, along the Afghan border. Whenever it gets too hot for the Taliban in Afghanistan, their units retire across the border, refit, and return when it suits them. While the Bush administration has put pressure on Musharraf to take the fight against the Taliban more seriously, Washington's main aim is to keep nuclear Pakistan broadly onside. If this means winking at Musharraf's game-playing with Taliban forces, so be it.

Despite praise from the Bush administration, President Musharraf remains ambivalent about his country's relationship with the United States, a stance that admirably suits the internal politics of his country. In his *60 Minutes* interview, he talked openly about the list of seven demands that Armitage had issued to the two Pakistani diplomats, and how he found two of them particularly irksome. One demand was for Pakistan to turn over its border posts and bases to the United States for use in the assault on the Taliban. The second demand, which Musharraf dismissed as ludicrous, was that Islamabad crack down on internal expressions of support for terrorist attacks on the United States. "If somebody's expressing views," Musharraf told CBS, "we cannot suppress the expression of views."[4] This was a tart statement of his position, deftly mirroring such utterances over the years from American leaders who lecture foreigners on the inability of Washington to suppress the free expression of views in the United States.

While Washington does not approve of Pakistan's ambivalence, it is not prepared to have a showdown over it with the Musharraf government. The United States has strategic interests in Pakistan that far exceed those in Afghanistan. Pakistan is a nuclear-weapons state that plays a crucial role in sustaining the balance of power in Asia with Russia, India, China, and Japan. Should the Musharraf government collapse in favour of a militant Islamic regime, the blow to Washington would be incalculable. The dual tactic of helping Musharraf stay in power in Islamabad, while keeping a gun to his head, has paid high dividends to the Americans, and they will not abandon it in the interest of NATO troops, even their own, fighting in southern Afghanistan. The beauty of Musharraf's position is that for the Americans he is the only game in town in Pakistan. While the Bush administration does not like the frank things he says, they need him just as much as the Pakistani president needs the Americans.

At the same time as Musharraf speaks plainly about the relationship of his country with the United States, he is involved in a desperate struggle to hold onto power. Not only is he engaged against his Islamist foes who would like to establish a theocratic regime, but he has also had to position himself vis-à-vis other political forces and avoid a calamitous showdown with the country's Supreme Court judges. In October 2007, while remaining in uniform, the general proceeded to contest an election for the country's presidency, although it was unclear whether the judges would let the election result stand. The election for the country's top post was held in Pakistan's two houses of parliament and in four provincial assemblies. In this electoral college contest, Musharraf won all but five votes in the two houses of parliament and swept the ballots in the provincial assemblies with huge majorities. While the Supreme Court judges did not block the vote, several legal challenges remained as to whether, as a general, Musharraf had a right to be a candidate.[5]

The political manoeuvring was a part of Musharraf's attempt to return his country to civilian rule with himself as president. The president made arrangements for loyal successors to take over the armed forces when he relinquished his uniform to become a civilian head of government—which he did on November 29, 2007, beginning a five-year term. Musharraf also entered into a compact with former prime minister Benazir Bhutto, dropping corruption charges against her, to allow her to return home from her self-imposed exile in London. The idea was that following parliamentary elections to be held in January 2008, the forces of Musharraf and Bhutto would co-operate in a power-sharing arrangement aimed at keeping the Islamists from power.

The planned shift to a normalized regime in Pakistan fell to tatters. Bhutto's return to the country on October 19 was met with a horrific terrorist attack. A throng of several hundred thousand people had come into the streets to line the route of her procession, and two giant bomb blasts in quick succession killed at least 126 people and wounded another 248. The procession was abandoned, and Bhutto was evacuated to her residence unharmed.[6]

On November 3 President Musharraf declared a state of emergency.[7] He suspended Pakistan's constitution, fired the chief justice of the Supreme Court, Iftikhar Muhammad Chaudry, and lined the streets of Islamabad with police officers. Musharraf's desperate move had multifold motives. For one thing, he faced the real possibility that the Supreme Court would nullify his election to the presidency prior to his stepping down as head of the armed forces. His crackdown was aimed widely at the judiciary and the country's leading lawyers, the centres from which arguments against his election as president were being mounted. Thousands of lawyers and judges were among those rounded up and imprisoned. In addition to the threat from lawyers and the judiciary, Musharraf was facing political challenges from a number of quarters. One of those arrested in the hours following the declaration of emergency rule was the leader of the party of exiled former prime minister Nawaz Sharif. In September 2007 Sharif had returned from exile for the first time after being ousted by Musharraf in a coup in 1999, only to be deported a few hours later. Former cricket star and politician Imran Khan was placed under house arrest. Speaking at a news conference at her residence in Karachi, Bhutto condemned the suspension of the constitution. As she put it, "If you really want to get rid of extremism, you have to get rid of dictatorship."[8]

To the United States and other Western countries, Musharraf explained the state of emergency as a measure aimed at fighting terrorism and extremism. While U.S. secretary of state Condoleezza Rice was quick to condemn Musharraf's move and to demand a "quick return to constitutional law,"[9] Washington was more fearful of a collapse into chaos in Pakistan than it was of martial law. A week after his proclaimed emergency, Musharraf told Pakistanis in a televised address that he planned to step down as head of the armed forces and to end the suspension of the constitution as soon as possible. He said the parliamentary elections scheduled for January 2008 would take place.

On December 27, 2007, Benazir Bhutto died at the hands of assassins in the streets of Rawalpindi, following an address to her supporters there. Her tragic death unleashed a wave of unrest in Pakistan, gravely deepening the crisis of legitimacy faced by the Musharraf regime. The crisis in Pakistan cast into clear relief what was truly important in the region from the viewpoint of the United States and the other Western powers. Compared to Pakistan, with its nuclear weapons, Afghanistan was small change. Keeping the Islamabad regime in one piece mattered far more to Washington than putting pressure on Musharraf to crack down on Taliban sanctuaries in the regions of Pakistan that bordered on Afghanistan.

In this game of smoke and mirrors, Canadian soldiers are engaged in a dirty war in which a supposed major ally in the region has been playing a duplicitous role. Washington is anxious to have NATO allies do as much of the difficult fighting as possible in southern Afghanistan, where the revitalized Taliban has been taking a toll. Not least, this is because the Bush administration needs to keep U.S. military casualties to a minimum, because American public opinion, already highly critical of the war, is negatively affected by rising casualties.

Canadian casualties, though, provoke no such reaction in the United States. The deaths of Canadian soldiers are rarely reported in the U.S. media. Should Canadians be paying a price in blood in a conflict in which double-dealing is the name of the game?

■ ■

This War Is Not about Human Rights

IN THE WEST THE AFGHAN WAR HAS BEEN WIDELY DEPICTED as a struggle between forces representing democracy and human rights, including the rights of women, on one side, and an authoritarian seventh-century-style theocracy on the other. While the Taliban regime was certainly ferociously anti-women in its policies, the record on the other side is far from being clean. In many parts of the country Afghan women remain severely restricted in their activities and girls are often not allowed to attend schools. Human rights reports over the last several years have documented a worsening situation for women in many parts of the country that are not under the control of the Taliban. The Kabul regime is far from liberal. When a man named Abdul Rahman was sentenced to death for converting to Christianity from Islam, his execution was stayed only in response to enraged public opinion in Western countries. The post-Taliban constitution in Afghanistan is based on Sharia law. Under the law, rejecting Islam is punishable by death.

The struggles in recent decades over who is to wield power in Afghanistan have had nothing to do with human rights. The Soviets invaded Afghanistan in 1979 to support a pro-Moscow regime that was in trouble. The Soviets intervened in Afghanistan for geostrategic reasons. They wanted to shore up the southern flank of their empire against potentially hostile forces. They were already concerned about the rise of militant Islamic movements and their potential to disrupt the Soviet Union itself, as indeed they were soon to do. Everywhere the Soviets went, from Eastern Europe to Africa, to Central and East Asia, they always talked about human rights and never practised them. It was not, therefore, unusual for the client Soviet regime in Kabul to promise human rights and national elections. For what it is worth, the Karmal government in Kabul was certainly less hostile to the idea of girls being educated and women working in various sectors of the economy than was the Mujahideen. Unlike the Taliban, which was one element among the Mujahideen, the pro-Soviet government did not require women to wear the burka.

The education of girls and the place of women in the workplace and in Afghan society have long been vexed questions in that country. Under its 1964 constitution Afghanistan was supposed to provide free and compulsory education at primary and secondary levels for males and females. This concept of schooling, based on Western models, did not deliver what it promised much if not most of the time. While Kabul and other larger towns had primary and secondary schools, in many parts of Afghanistan, which is about 70 per cent rural, no schools existed at all. Nonetheless, there was education for girls, delivered in this highly uneven fashion. During the decades of war prior to, during, and after the Soviet occupation, and in the subsequent struggle that propelled the Taliban into power, the educational system was ravaged. Tens of thousands of educated Afghans fled the country. Then, of course, the Taliban came to power and abolished education for girls and drove women out of the workplace.

Today education for girls and the right of women to work have been re-established, both in principle and to some extent in practice. In Kabul and other large cities, girls attend school and women can be employed outside the home. In the countryside, however, little has changed. Women work in the fields and homes, and few girls attend school. That was the case before and during the Taliban regime, and it remains the case today. In the country as a whole, about one-third of girls now attend school, and most boys do. This puts Afghanistan back where it was on this issue in pre-Taliban days. Today about 51 per cent of males and 21 per cent of females in Afghanistan are literate.

The West is clearly not on the side of the angels in Afghanistan. After all, when the Carter administration took up the cause of the insurgents against the Soviet client regime in Kabul—Carter often talked about injecting concern for human rights into U.S. foreign policy—he aligned the United States with the Mujahideen, the forces in Afghanistan that not only had no interest whatsoever in democracy but were also the most repressive element on the issue of women's rights, and the education of girls. In addition, the U.S. government had no particular difficulty with the Taliban after it came to power. Regarding the Taliban as potentially useful in the region against other players, Washington continued to provide aid to the Taliban regime in Kabul as late as four months prior to the September 11 attacks.

The two sides in the civil war in Afghanistan pit tribal and regional power groupings, including those disaffected due to the crackdown on poppy growing, against one another. A major complication is that the country remains the centre of the world's opium and heroin trade. Much of the resistance to the West's intervention has nothing to do with the Taliban, or al Qaeda for that matter, but has been provoked by the insistence of the Americans and the British that poppy cultivation—the main source of income in much of the country—must be halted. (The former Taliban regime also worked to reduce the drug trade, but now the insurgents, including the Taliban, are using the resentment of poppy growers—and funds from them—to sustain their cause.)

Since the U.S. invasion in 2001, poppy production in Afghanistan has skyrocketed. A U.S. State Department official estimated that in 2005 Afghanistan was the source of 86 per cent of the world's heroin. The same source reported that poppy production increased appreciably in 2006. In a country with one of the lowest living standards in the world, in which about 80 per cent of the workforce is unemployed, the opium trade is the major backbone of the productive economy. The highly organized international drug cartel has close ties with corrupt local officials, who profit handsomely from the drug trade, as well as with elements in the Taliban.

In a fine piece of reporting from Afghanistan in *The New Yorker* in July 2007, Jon Lee Anderson made the case that the struggle in that country has become the "Taliban's opium war."[1] In 2005 the government of Hamid Karzai announced that it would wage a struggle against the opium trade and that the goals of the campaign would include building the justice system to eliminate corruption, eradicating the poppy crop, and providing viable crop alternatives for farmers displaced in the war on the poppy. Some two years into the campaign, backed by billions of dollars in aid from the United States for this effort, the Kabul government had achieved little.

The tangled struggle over opium by no means pits the Kabul government against the Taliban and the poppy growers in a straight-forward way. Many of those involved in the opium trade have very close ties to the government. For example, there have been persistent allegations that Hamid Karzai's brother, Ahmed Wali Karzai, who is based in Kandahar, is a major participant in the drug trade. Taj Mohammad Wardak, a former minister of the interior, told *The Guardian*, "If you ask people in the bazaar [in Kandahar], four out of ten will tell you that Karzai's brother is exporting drugs." (Karzai's brother denies the allegations.)[2]

Among the methods used by the United States to wage war on the poppy crop has been to contract out the work to private corporations such as Virginia-based Dyn-Corp, a military company that has signed numerous contracts with the U.S. government to do work for it in Iraq and Colombia. Dyn-Corp has been under contract to receive a share of the multi-billion-dollar payout to implement Plan Colombia, the drug war whose goal is to eradicate Colombia's coca crop. In Afghanistan the company provides a force of heavily armed contract operatives—a private army—whose members work alongside the U.S. military to undertake forays into the countryside to destroy the poppies in the fields.

The Taliban, while in power, achieved a substantial reduction of the poppy crop. Now that it is at the centre of the counter-insurgency, however, the Taliban has become a major backer of the poppy growers and opium merchants. As Lieutenant-General Mohammad Daud-Daud, deputy minister of counter-narcotics in Afghanistan, explained to Anderson, "There has been a coalition between the Taliban and the opium smugglers. This year, they have set up a commission to tax the harvest." The Taliban has provided the poppy farmers with protection from the Afghan-U.S. campaign to destroy their crops. The Taliban's strategy has won it revenue for arms and supplies and political support in important farming regions.

For his *New Yorker* article Anderson went on a harrowing journey into the countryside in the heart of Taliban country, accompanying Dyn-Corp men and U.S. troops on a poppy-eradication mission. The foray was made in Uruzgan province in the central part of the country. The Taliban effectively controlled 80 per cent of the province, whose population is largely Pashtun. Leader Mullah Omar was born in Uruzgan.

NATO's military operations in the province have been run by the Dutch, whose low-profile approach has kept their troops largely confined to their heavily armed base. The Dutch believe that the key to success in this region is to provide aid for reconstruction efforts and to ignore the Taliban as much as possible. The effect of this soft approach, very much at odds with that of the United States, and the Canadians for that matter, has been to render the Taliban irrelevant in the eyes of the local population. The Americans' approach is to believe that by invading the countryside and destroying the poppies, they will teach the farmers that growing the crop is no dependable way to make a living and that the Taliban cannot be counted on for protection.

Understandably, given these conflicting views, the foray that Anderson witnessed did not elicit much sympathy or backing from the Dutch military; and the expedition could not be counted much of a success. Some poppies were destroyed in the fields, to the annoyance of the farmers involved, and a vicious firefight occurred between the U.S./ Dyn-Corp units and the Taliban, but the U.S. strategy in general has left the Taliban's hold on much of the countryside, and its farmers, substantially unscathed.

The war in Afghanistan is in large measure a struggle about the future of the world's leading narco-state. A clear-cut struggle between good guys and bad guys, this is not.

For Canadians, the point that the war was not a struggle for human rights was driven home in the early months of 2007 by revelations that the Canadian forces in Afghanistan had been handing over captured insurgents to the Afghan authorities only to have them tortured. In a series of articles that shone the spotlight on the issue, *The Globe and Mail* created a political firestorm for the Harper government.

From the early days of Canada's military mission in Afghanistan, the military had advised the government that the task of building and running Canadian detention facilities to house captured insurgents was prohibitively expensive and beyond the military's existing expertise. The practice, therefore, was to turn prisoners over to the Americans or the Karzai government. The trouble with handing prisoners over to the Americans is that many of them could end up being transferred to the U.S. facility in Guantanamo Bay in Cuba. If the prisoners were dispatched to the Afghans, what guarantee would Canada have that they would not be mistreated?

In 2005 Bill Graham, Canada's minister of National Defence, became concerned about the issue and badly wanted to reach an agreement on detainees with the Afghan authorities. The minister sought a transfer arrangement that would specify that detainees turned over by Canada would enjoy Geneva Convention rights. The deal would have to include an understanding that both Canada and Afghanistan would maintain written files on all prisoners, and that the prisoners could be visited by the International Committee of the Red Cross (ICRC) and by the Karzai government's Afghan Independent Human Rights Commission.

As it turned out, the deal with the Afghans was only reached in December 2005 by General Hillier, chief of defence staff, who signed the understanding with Afghanistan's defence minister, Abdul Rahim Wardak, in Kabul.[3] While the deal finalized by the general included the stipulations that Graham had wanted, it was to prove disastrously inadequate. Unlike agreements signed with the Afghans by other NATO countries, including the Netherlands and the United Kingdom, Canada's agreement contained no stipulation that Canada could follow up on transferred detainees to ensure that they were not being tortured in Afghan prisons. By the time the deal was signed, the federal election that would bring Harper's Conservatives to office was underway, and it was the Harper government that would be roiled by the fallout in early 2007.

Evidence mounted that prisoners in Afghan hands were being mistreated. In *The Unexpected War*, Stein and Lang report that the Afghan Independent Human Rights Commission, Amnesty International, and Canadian Louise Arbour, the UN Commissioner for Human Rights, "had concluded that abuse, torture, and extrajudicial killing were routinely inflicted on people in Afghan custody."[4]

Pointing the finger directly at the Canadian government was University of Ottawa law professor Amir Attaran. Using the federal *Access to Information Act*, Professor Attaran obtained documents from which he concluded that Afghan detainees appear to have been beaten while detained and interrogated by Canadian soldiers. The professor used this information to request an investigation into the treatment of the detainees by the Military Police Complaints Commission, a civilian body established to investigate complaints against the Canadian military. In light of these allegations, in February 2007, the Canadian military launched investigations into the matter of detainee abuse by Canadian soldiers in Afghanistan.[5]

The allegations brought to light by Professor Attaran stemmed from an incident in April 2006 when Canadian soldiers captured three Afghans. The heavily redacted record that Professor Attaran obtained through Access to Information referred to injuries sustained by the prisoners while they were under Canadian custody. Subsequently the three men were handed over to the Afghans. In the winter of 2007, when officers from the Canadian Forces National Investigation Service set out to talk to the men about the allegations that they had been injured while in Canadian custody, the men could not be found.

The Globe and Mail continued to unearth information that heightened the pressure on the Harper government. A *Globe* reporter managed to find and interview thirty former detainees who said they had been transferred from Canadian to Afghan jurisdiction and then tortured while in Afghan hands.[6] While these allegations could not be independently verified, a powerful case was being made that Canada had turned over prisoners with little thought for their fate and that the government had tried to cover up its own shoddy performance.

Making matters much worse for Ottawa was the performance of Defence Minister Gordon O'Connor in the House of Commons. On the matter of the treatment of detainees handed over to the Afghans, the minister told MPs that the International Committee of the Red Cross was monitoring the condition of these detainees. In May 2006 O'Connor declared in the Commons: "The Red Cross or the Red Crescent is responsible to supervise their treatment once the prisoners are in the hands of the Afghan authorities. If there is something wrong with their treatment, the Red Cross or Red Crescent would inform us and we would take action."[7]

In early March 2007 the rug was pulled out from under that position when Simon Schorno, a spokesperson for the ICRC, told *The Globe and Mail,* "We were informed of the agreement, but we are not a party to it and we are not monitoring the implementation of it." On March 19, 2007, O'Connor apologized to the House of Commons for the misleading statements he had made on the issue. "I fully and without reservation apologize to the House for providing inaccurate information for members," he said, adding, "The International Red Cross Committee is under no obligation to share information with Canada on the treatment of detainees transferred by Canada to Afghan authorities."[8]

To staunch the public relations and political calamity that had befallen them, the Harper government rushed to conclude a new agreement with the Karzai government on May 3, 2007. On paper at least, the new agreement contained additional protections for transferred detainees. Under its terms, representatives of Canada were to be accorded unfettered access to the prisoners, including the right to hold private interviews with them.[9]

That seemed to be the end of the matter, but not quite. As Stein and Lang point out, Ahmad Fahim Hakim, the deputy chair of the Afghanistan Independent Human Rights Commission, told them that the Commission could not guarantee that prisoners were not being tortured in Afghan detention centres. The Commission, he said, had too few monitors, and could take up to twenty days after being notified of a problem to pay a first visit to a detainee.[10]

The detainee issue returned with a vengeance in autumn 2007. On November 16 *The Globe and Mail* reported that, according to newly released documents, the Harper government "knew prison conditions were appalling" well before the newspaper published accounts the previous spring "detailing the abuse and torture of prisoners turned over by Canadian soldiers to Afghanistan's notorious secret police." According to the *Globe*, "The heavily censored documents also show that at the same time as senior ministers were denying evidence of abuse, officials on the ground in Afghanistan were collecting first-hand accounts from prisoners of mistreatment."

Well before the public allegations that prisoners were being abused and tortured, Canadian officials were reporting to Ottawa on the terrible state of the prison conditions. In February 2007, for instance, Linda Garwood-Filbert, the head of a Correctional Service Canada inspections team, requested better boots because she was "walking through blood and fecal matter" on the floor of cells during tours of Afghan prisons.[11]

■ ■

Appalling and massive human rights violations, unfortunately, seem to be the norm in Afghanistan—from the Taliban government to their opponents in the Northern Alliance, with whom the United States made common cause in the autumn of 2001. During the struggle that resulted in the Taliban taking power in 1996 and after that date, members of the Northern Alliance perpetrated well-documented abuses, including warfare that indiscriminately targeted civilians, the burning of houses, torture, looting, and rape. Summary executions were sometimes carried out in front of victims' relatives, and children under the age of fifteen were recruited to fight against the Taliban. Ethnic Pashtuns, who formed the largest base of support for the Taliban, were frequently the targets of these abuses. In January 1997, aircraft controlled by one faction of the Northern Alliance dropped cluster bombs on residential districts of Kabul. Later that year, about three thousand Taliban troops were summarily executed in and around Mazare Sharif when the town fell into the hands of anti-Taliban forces. A 1996 U.S. State Department report on human rights abuses in 1995 found that when forces of the Jamiat-I Islami (a Northern Alliance faction), under the command of Ahmad Shah Massoud, captured a neighbourhood in Kabul, "Massoud's troops went on a rampage, systemically looting whole streets, and raping women."[12] (Massoud was killed in a suicide bomb attack two days before the September 11, 2001, terror attacks.)

The sad truth about the human rights issue in Afghanistan is that it has always been trumpeted by foreigners who intervene in the country, not as a way of appealing to Afghans, but as a way of bringing their own people on side. Westerners will have no difficulty appreciating this in the case of the Soviets, whose human rights record was abominable, both at home and abroad. To make the case to the world communist movement that the Soviet Union was on the progressive side, the Soviets always made much of their belief in the rights of women, in the rule of law, and free elections. On the latter two points, Soviet propaganda was almost always the exact reverse of the truth. On the issue of women's rights, the Soviets, who were anti-religious, were no more inclined to discriminate against women than they were against men. In that negative sense, the Soviet client regime in Kabul was a boon to women, certainly in comparison to the regime that came afterward, with its U.S. backing.

The U.S. attack on Afghanistan in autumn 2001 was not provoked by the Taliban record on human rights, miserable though it was, but by the terror attacks on New York and Washington. The decision of the Bush administration to invade Afghanistan grew out of the anger of Americans in the aftermath of the September 11 attacks. Even as that attack unfolded, the key members of the administration were already thinking ahead to the next and larger conflict, the invasion of Iraq. But from the beginning the Bush administration trumpeted the human rights issue as a central feature of its global War on Terror.

The portrait of the world that Bush painted in the weeks following September 11 was etched in black and white. Al Qaeda had attacked New York and Washington because the terrorists hated the freedom that Americans enjoyed and wanted to snuff it out. This line of argument became the watchword of the administration. The world was divided between the friends of liberty and its foes, and America was the global leader of the friends of liberty. In his second inaugural address in January 2005, Bush took this to extremes when he declared,

"America, in this young century, proclaims liberty throughout all the world and to all the inhabitants thereof."[13]

Sadly, for the Iraqis and Afghans, the president's edict delivered little apart from death, ruin, and fear.

The human rights question in Afghanistan does not solely turn on the records of successive Afghan regimes and political groupings. It also has to do with the behaviour of occupying forces in the country. The Soviets sowed ruin and destruction in Afghanistan during their years as an occupying force. The Americans, notwithstanding the insistence of the Bush administration that it stands on the side of liberty, have been responsible for one of the great human rights atrocities of this new century—the holding of prisoners captured in Afghanistan at the U.S. detainment camp in Guantanamo, Cuba. That camp, operated since 2002 at the U.S. Naval Base in Guantanamo, houses prisoners captured in Afghanistan whom U.S. authorities claim are Taliban and al Qaeda operatives. The Bush administration insisted that the Guantanamo detainees were "enemy combatants," not soldiers of a regular military force, and that, therefore, they were not entitled to the treatment accorded to military prisoners under the Geneva conventions. In June 2006, the U.S. Supreme Court ruled that the administration's notion of the status of the prisoners was invalid. The following month, the U.S. Defense Department issued a memo indicating that henceforth the prisoners would be accorded treatment as specified under the Geneva conventions.[14]

Of the original 775 detainees, 340 have been released, and 110 others are said to be about to be released. Another 70 or more prisoners will face trial, leaving about 250 prisoners who could be held indefinitely. Since the detainees were first housed at Guantanamo, there have been widespread calls for the facility to be shut down. It is alleged that prisoners in the camp have been tortured, their religion has been insulted, their legal rights denied, and that they have been denied visits from outside agencies.[15]

The record of his administration aside, Bush's liberty pledge was more than a mere exercise in bombast. It was aimed at widening public support in the United States and elsewhere in the West for the missions in Afghanistan and Iraq. Rhetorically at least, Bush was aligning himself with the American liberal tradition, with its deep attachment to freedom. Bush's crusade for liberty did succeed in bringing on board a group of intellectuals generally regarded as liberals. One of these, Michael Ignatieff, now the deputy leader of the Liberal Party, supported both of the Bush invasions. Ignatieff portrayed the United States as an "Empire Lite." As he wrote in his book of that title, "The 21st century imperium is a new invention in the annals of political science ... a global hegemony whose grace notes are free markets, human rights and democracy, enforced by the most awesome military power the world has ever known." On Afghanistan, he observed, "It is at least ironic that liberal believers ... someone like me, for example—can end up supporting the creation of a new humanitarian empire, a new form of colonial tutelage for the peoples of Kosovo, Bosnia and Afghanistan." In January 2003, before the invasion of Iraq, Ignatieff wrote in *The New York Times Magazine*, "The case for empire is that it has become, in a place like Iraq, the last hope for democracy and stability alike." (In August 2007, again writing in *The New York Times Magazine*, Ignatieff concluded that he had been wrong in supporting the U.S.-led invasion of Iraq.)[16]

This "missionary position" has been adopted by thinkers such as Ignatieff who have been stirred to passion by the drive to remake the Middle East and Central Asia according to American values. In a narrative that the emperor Hadrian would have understood, these new liberal imperialists warn that the civilized world is threatened by barbarians who lash out at it for a variety of reasons. Exploiting the situation in "failed states," where human catastrophes brought on by civil war, natural disaster, disease, genocide, and religious persecution have destroyed the possibility of viable states, the enemies of civilization take root. In the world's string of failed states, which can be likened to the asteroid belt between Mars and Jupiter where planets failed to form, drug smugglers, traffickers in human chattels, and terrorists have set up shop. From these safe havens, they lash out at the rest of the world. Most dangerous in our age of instant communications and weapons of mass destruction are the terrorists, with al Qaeda the generic name for terrorists committed to Islamic fundamentalism, those dangerous souls who have the capacity to strike the First World as fiercely or more fiercely as they did on September 11.

In *Longitudes and Attitudes*, prolific author and *New York Times* columnist Thomas Friedman states it frankly: "How the World of Order deals with the World of Disorder is the key question of the day."[17] Friedman's argument is that to make the world safe the forces of civilization, led by the United States, must strike at the sanctuaries of the barbarians, just as the Romans did in their time.

The people of Afghanistan have long been the victims of outside powers. Like the previous invasions of Afghanistan, the U.S. assault in autumn 2001 was driven by motives that had nothing to do with the human rights of the people of that country. When the geostrategic wheel shifts and U.S. interests push them in a different direction with rethought priorities, the rhetorical concern for human rights in Afghanistan will also vanish.

The conflict in Afghanistan is a civil war. The West's armies are ranged on one side. In Afghanistan Canadians are not fighting against an external invasion or even against the invasion of one part of a country by another, as was the case in the Korean War in the early 1950s. Does it make sense for Canada to send its troops into harm's way thousands of kilometres from home in such a conflict?

One clear-eyed observer of Afghanistan is Eric Margolis, the Canadian foreign policy analyst who has spent a great deal of time in Central Asia and has written widely on the issue. His book *War at the Top of the World* should be required reading on the subject.[18] In a spring 2006 article, "Three Big Lies about Afghanistan," Margolis wrote that "most foreign journalists" don't see the truth behind the government and military handouts about the struggle for democracy and human rights in Afghanistan. "They get the Cook's tour," he wrote, "led around by their noses by government or military P.R. specialists, and fed handouts. Call this blinkered news.... Few reporters get away from the military and go see the reality beyond. Even fewer know about Afghanistan's tortured history. That's why we have been getting so much disinformation and so little honest reporting about Afghanistan."[19]

■ ■

[handwritten note: → similar to Hart?]

The United States Is Losing the Wider War

FOR THE UNITED STATES, AFGHANISTAN IS THE SIDESHOW. Iraq is the main event. The staying power of the United States in Afghanistan will largely be determined by what happens in Iraq. If Americans—elites and ordinary people alike—decide that Iraq is a lost cause, they will soon decide the same thing about Afghanistan. A U.S. troop withdrawal from Iraq will quickly be followed by a withdrawal from Afghanistan. When Canadians consider the future of their Afghan mission, they need to keep an eye on Iraq. What happens there will determine the geostrategic outlook for Afghanistan.

While the Harper government prefers that Canadians not think about Iraq and Afghanistan in the same breath, the reality is that even though the Afghan mission operates under NATO command and UN auspices, the U.S. invasion was its starting point. Should the Americans decide to leave or dramatically scale back their mission, the rest of the West will not remain long in the country.

Quite apart from its invasion of Afghanistan, the U.S. government is engaged in a strategic struggle to establish hegemony in the vital region of the Persian Gulf (home to 60 per cent of the world's proven petroleum reserves) as well as in Central Asia, including Afghanistan and Pakistan. This whole region is now the scene of a wider war being conducted on a number of fronts. America's ally Israel is embroiled in conflict with elements of the Palestinian Authority in Gaza and the West Bank, and fought a brief war in Lebanon in the summer of 2006. The United States and the members of the "coalition of the willing" are fighting in Iraq in a mission that is increasingly being depicted as a disaster by U.S. and British intelligence, as well as by highly placed military officials in Washington and London. The United States is determined to block Iran from acquiring nuclear weapons. A U.S. aerial assault on Iran's nuclear facilities could be the next phase in an even wider war. Conflict is raging in Afghanistan, especially in the regions of the country that border on Pakistan. Meanwhile, the U.S. missions in this region of the world are being subjected to increasing scrutiny in elite circles, as well as among the American people at large.

Some four years or more after the invasion of the country by the "coalition of the willing," Iraq is embroiled in a civil war. The execution of Saddam Hussein on December 30, 2006, cast into clear relief the divisions within the country. In Shiite and Kurdish districts of Iraq, celebrants took to the streets, firing guns in the air and cheering the death of the former tyrant. In the Sunni heartland, where Saddam was buried, hundreds came out to mourn him, vowing revenge for the hanging of their leader. The American occupiers have been reduced almost to the level of spectators as sectarian violence drives Iraq towards balkanization. Political elders—Republican James Baker and Democrat Lee Hamilton—were called in as co-chairs of the Iraq Study Group to seek a graceful way out of Iraq for the Bush administration. Disillusioned with the war and the broader foreign policy vision of the administration, U.S. voters punished the Republicans when they handed control of both houses of Congress to the Democrats in the November 2006 elections.

In December 2006 both the Baker-Hamilton Report (*Report of the Iraq Study Group*)[1] and Defense Secretary Designate Robert Gates, in testimony before Congress, declared what had been unthinkable in Republican circles—that the United States was not winning the war in Iraq. The Baker-Hamilton Report not only advocated a withdrawal of U.S. troops from Iraq sometime in 2008, but also called for negotiations with Syria and Iran, leading states that, according to Bush administration orthodoxy, sponsor terror. When he released his report, James Baker, a patrician elder statesman from the Bush Sr. administration, reminded the media that it had been American policy to talk to foes during the more than four decades of the Cold War.

The Baker-Hamilton Report was a clear signal that an important rift had opened up within the U.S. political establishment, not just about the Iraq war but about the approach of the United States to global issues. On one side of the debate is the Bush administration, committed to the neo-conservative conception of the American global mission. On the other side are the so-called "realists." The Baker-Hamilton Report represents a statement of their views.

The neo-conservative school of American foreign policy has promoted a radicalization of America's global stance. Not satisfied with the status quo in which America is the strongest power, the neo-conservatives have set out to increase the country's global supremacy. At the centre of their global mission has been the struggle in the Middle East and Central Asia. During the halcyon days of the Bush administration in the aftermath of September 11, the use of military power was seen as the crucial way to transform societies with regimes hostile to Washington. War could be used as the means for creating democratic, liberal societies in countries such as Afghanistan and Iraq. Along with the drive to export an American-style version of liberty to other countries, the Bush administration proclaimed its determination to ensure that the United States remain the world's dominant military power, able to face down challenges from friendly and hostile regimes alike.

The Bush administration's global policies were based both on a utopian drive to foster foreign regimes that were rooted in American values and on a fundamentalist impulse to combat evil. In a conversation with Palestinian prime minister Mahmoud Abbas in 2003, Bush proclaimed: "God told me to strike al Qaeda and I struck them, and then he instructed me to strike at Saddam, which I did."

By the end of 2006 the Bush administration's policies were in tatters in the failing wars in Iraq and Afghanistan, in relationships with many countries around the world, and in the rising crisis caused by America's inability to finance its military operations and keep its fiscal house in order. In Iraq the political and military strategies of the administration were both exposed as completely threadbare. Far from being received as liberators in the country, the American occupiers provoked not only a massive and growing resistance to their presence, but also a deep internecine conflict among the elements that made up Iraqi society. Sunnis and Shiites were at each other's throats, and the city of Baghdad, where both elements were present, was reduced to a warren of warring neighbourhoods. In Baghdad local militias were defending their own turf, and the central authority was unable to establish any semblance of law and order. Thousands of people—those who had the means to do so—were fleeing the city every week. The planners of the invasion had utterly failed to predict the kind of calamity that would descend on the society as a consequence of their overthrow of the Saddam Hussein regime. Having destroyed the existing Iraqi state, the Americans had nothing they could replace it with.

Contributing to the chaos in Iraq was the U.S. military doctrine, espoused by the U.S. Department of Defense under Donald Rumsfeld. Rumsfeld, Vice-President Dick Cheney, and other neo-conservative stalwarts had used Iraq as a proving ground for their theory of warfare. Ignoring the advice and warnings of Pentagon generals that Iraq could only be pacified with a much larger American and allied occupation force, Rumsfeld had insisted that a force of about 140,000 U.S. troops could get the job done.

Although things appeared to go well for the Americans in Iraq for the first few months, by the end of 2003 and certainly by the end of 2004 the writing was on the wall for the Rumsfeld strategy. The U.S. occupying force was too small. The generals were right and Rumsfeld was wrong, and it was not a mistake that could easily be corrected. The U.S. Army had been reshaped according to the Rumsfeld doctrine. Changing it would require a long period of reorganization and vastly increased military expenditures. In the meantime, Iraq had passed the point of no return. By the end of 2006 a much larger occupying force, which might have been effective against the insurgency and the descent into sectarian violence two or three years earlier, could no longer do the job. The horses had long since escaped from the barn.

With the strategy of the Bush administration in disarray, the door was open to the alternative doctrines of the realist school. James Baker is famed for his genteel manner. Beneath his smiling exterior, however, there is not a sentimental bone in his body. He is interested in the global power of the United States and making the world safe for American enterprise. He will consort with the devil to realize these ambitions. The Baker-Hamilton Report discarded the establishment of democracy in Iraq as a major objective. What these elders wanted was pacification in the Persian Gulf. If they had to sup with unpleasant people to achieve that, no problem. Baker was prepared to treat with the governments of Iran and Syria, not because he liked them, but because they exercised power in the region. Keep your friends close and your enemies closer: this could be his motto.

The realists aspire to making deals where necessary. Their goal is to maintain a global, and in the Middle East, regional order, in which U.S. geopolitical and business interests are paramount. To achieve their objectives, the realists are not inclined to make outsize sacrifices on behalf of Israel, as the neo-conservatives have been prepared to do. Baker and the realists are quite content with the regime in Saudi Arabia, medieval though it prefers to remain.

The realist outlook on Iraq is bound to spread to the lesser conflict in Afghanistan as well. An important wrinkle in the Afghanistan conflict, one that has been kept as much as possible from Canadian eyes, is the pro-Taliban stance taken by much of the Pakistani state apparatus. The Bakerites, and other realists, are bound to show as little interest in democracy and women's rights in Afghanistan as they have in Iraq. In sharp contrast to the good versus evil simplicities that we have been sold on Afghanistan, the Pakistanis, for tribal, regional, and geopolitical reasons, are certain to go on backing Pashtun and other southern Afghan groupings, whatever their ideology. The apparatchiks of the Pakistan state, as little interested in democracy and women's rights as are Baker's friends in Saudi Arabia, are never going to do more than genuflect in the direction of George W. Bush's War on Terror.

Should it come time for the U.S. realists to make peace in Afghanistan, they will happily help cobble together a new regime, comprising elements of the Taliban, the old Northern Alliance, and assorted drug dealers and war lords. This will all be done, too, without a thought for Stephen Harper, the editorial writers of the *National Post*, and other neo-conservative media outlets. How long Hamid Karzai will survive as head of government in this situation is hard to say, but we can be sure that the ideals of democracy, the rule of law, rights for non-Muslims, and school for females will all receive short shrift.

In September 2007 details became public about the latest attempts of the Karzai government to reach a deal with elements of the Taliban. Karzai said that he would be prepared to meet personally with Mullah Omar, considered by the United States to be one of the world's most-wanted terrorists, to offer members of the insurgency positions in his government. The offer put U.S. and Canadian officials in a difficult position. Having made the case that the leaders of the

Taliban were the enemies of women's rights and the rule of law, how could they explain to the public in their own countries that Karzai was prepared to bring these very people into his government? How would Americans and Canadians feel about putting their young men and women in harm's way to strengthen Karzai's ability to restructure his government by adding to it elements that might favour reintroducing the harshly misogynist policies of the Taliban?

Kurt Volker, the deputy head of the European and Eurasian Affairs Office at the U.S. State Department, stated that Washington welcomed the Afghan president's overture to foes to negotiate, provided they rejected violence.[2] Canada's Foreign Affairs minister, Maxime Bernier, said that while it is up to the Karzai government to decide "how and with whom to engage in order to bring sustainable peace" to Afghanistan, "we hope that negotiations will only be conducted with individuals and organizations that will respect human rights and renounce violence."[3] The tentative language used here was a far cry from the accusations in the fall of 2006 that the NDP's Layton was being "naive" in advocating peace talks with the Taliban.

The struggle for power between the neo-conservatives and the realists in the United States is by no means over. The Bush administration, while on the defensive, continues to have warlike ambitions in the Middle East and Central Asia. The neo-conservatives in Washington and the Israeli government have been keeping a wary eye on Iran as a potential threat in the region—a threat that could be countered by an aerial assault on the country. The pretext for such an assault would be the refusal of the Iranian government to give up its plans to develop a nuclear program, plans allegedly made for the purpose of generating nuclear power. The Bush administration and nuclear-armed Israel (the best estimate is that Israel possesses about two hundred nuclear missiles) continued to argue in autumn 2007 that Iran was determined to produce nuclear weapons, despite a report by all sixteen U.S. intelligence agencies that Iran had, as early as 2003, dropped its program to produce a nuclear weapon.[4]

For the neo-conservatives, who see their power draining away, the prospect of an air war against Iran's nuclear facilities and its military-industrial complexes is tempting. Thwarted in Iraq and Afghanistan in lengthy ground wars, which have become highly unpopular with the American people, some (the Cheney faction of the administration, for example) were seeing the prospect of an air war in which U.S. power can be displayed to maximum effect as a way of propelling the Americans to victory in the larger regional struggle.

On January 7, 2007, the *Sunday Times of London* reported that Israeli pilots had been training to carry out a pinpoint attack on three Iranian targets that are believed to house nuclear facilities and uranium enrichment sites.[5] The *Sunday Times* said that Israeli planes had been flying to Gibraltar to practise for the 3,000-kilometre return flight to Iran, possibly by way of Turkey. The story included speculation from unnamed Israeli military sources that to destroy facilities housed many metres underground, the Israelis could use low-yield nuclear weapons.

Spokespersons for the Israeli government responded tartly that they don't comment on articles in the *Sunday Times*. The *Sunday Times* story ran just over a week before Dr. Mohammad Al Baradi, the chief of the International Atomic Energy Agency, visited Paris and warned in a television interview that Iran could be in a position to produce a nuclear weapon within three years.

Meanwhile, in Washington, leading Democratic senators John D. Rockefeller IV of West Virginia, Senate majority leader Harry Reid of Nevada, and Joseph Biden of Delaware have been warning Americans that the Bush administration is preparing public opinion for an attack on Iran at a time when the United States does not possess the military resources for such an attack, does not have the support of its allies, and does not have the backing of Congress.

In the aftermath of the November 2006 Congressional elections and the report of the Iraq Study Group, the Bush administration decided on its course in Iraq for the coming year. In an address to the American people on January 10, 2007, the president announced that the United States would dispatch an additional 21,500 troops to Iraq,[6] a reinforcement whose purpose was to try to halt the descent into chaos, particularly in Baghdad. The mission of the troops was to go into Baghdad's toughest neighbourhoods. Holding out hope that yet more force could do the job, Bush said that in the past "there were too many restrictions on the troops we did have," and that this time "we will have the force levels we need to hold the areas that have been cleared." Although the tone was far less vainglorious than in previous speeches on the war, Bush held out the hope that "victory will bring something new in the Arab world—a functioning democracy that polices its territory, upholds the rule of law, respects fundamental human liberties, and answers to its people." The real emphasis in the speech was not on remaking the Middle East, but on bloodying the noses of the insurgents and strengthening the Iraqi government so that the United States could hand over the security job to the Iraqis.

The new Bush strategy fell between two stools. For neo-con-servatives, those who remain committed to the idea of persevering to achieve victory in Iraq, the additional troops were not enough. They wanted fifty thousand or more reinforcements to crush the insurgency, and they wanted a commitment that the troops would stay until victory was achieved. At the other end of the political spectrum were those who wanted a firm commitment that U.S. troops would begin coming home soon. Americans have been migrating towards this position on the war for some time. Most Americans were no longer in a mood to be aroused by stirring words about liberating the Iraqis. They wanted out of the conflict as soon as a decent departure could be managed.

Not enough of a reinforcement to please the neo-cons and not a clear enough commitment to pull out of Iraq to please the majority of Americans—that was the awkward position in which the president found himself.

It is not as though the world has never witnessed anything like this in the past. What is happening is very similar to the American stance in Vietnam in the last two years before the North Vietnamese and the National Liberation Front seized Saigon in 1975. When Richard Nixon was elected president in 1968, his mandate was ambiguous—he pledged to get Americans out of a war they had come to detest, while still promising to win it. In office, Nixon tried to achieve victory by broadening the conflict into Cambodia and Laos, which was all for naught. The Nixon White House came to the view—with an important input from the great realist of the day, Henry Kissinger—that the United

States had to make a deal with North Vietnam to allow it to withdraw from the war, and further that it had to make an opening to China, to further divide the Communist superpowers, the Soviet Union and China, against each other. On the road to the deal with North Vietnam, which was signed in 1973, the emphasis from Washington was to bring about the "Vietnamization" of the war. The idea of Vietnamization was that U.S. units would progressively withdraw from their fighting role and that South Vietnamese units would take their place. The U.S. role would then limit itself to training the South Vietnamese forces. Following elections in South Vietnam, the question was whether the regime there could survive without being powerfully supported by tens of thousands of U.S. soldiers.

In the end, of course, South Vietnam collapsed, and the American presence in the country came to an end. The U.S. defeat in the war did not, however, lead to a collapse of the country's position in Southeast Asia, as many had forecast. The dominoes, as the countries in the region had been called, did not fall. These countries did not follow Vietnam into the Communist camp. Instead, something that was quite unforeseen only a few years earlier transpired. The Nixon administration made its historic opening to China, with the president visiting Beijing. Having insisted in the past that the Communist world was a single juggernaut that must be resisted as such, a Republican administration faced reality and took advantage of the chasm of mistrust that had grown up between Beijing and Moscow. The new strategy aimed at balancing off the two Communist giants by drawing closer to each in different ways.

The new approach bore fruit for the Americans. It played an important part in increasing the pressure on the Soviet Union and its empire that contributed to the demise of this superpower, a decade and a half after the United States withdrew in disarray from the U.S. embassy in Saigon in 1975. Moreover, the overture to China played a key role in pushing the world's largest country down the road to a vast economic opening to capitalism and the West. Over the longer term, the Americans were helping to create their next imperial challenger, but that is another story.

As for Vietnam, the victorious Communist forces soon found themselves in a shooting war against the hostile Chinese on their northern border. The Vietnamese had won an unimaginable victory against an immense foe, but Vietnam remained a poor and devastated country. It would not be too many years before the government in Hanoi wanted to throw the door open to foreign investment, including U.S. investment.

The American soldiers who had fought to halt the spread of Communism and to help construct a democratic South Vietnam came home. They never were awarded a tickertape parade in New York City. But eventually the Americans who died in the war that should never have been fought were remembered in the most poignant of the monuments in Washington, D.C., the wall where the names of the thousands who perished were recorded.

Bush's decision to send more troops to Iraq should not be interpreted as a determination on the part of Washington to fight through to final victory. Indeed, Bush hinted at that in his speech when he said, "Victory will not look like the ones our fathers and grandfathers achieved. There will be no surrender ceremony on the deck of a battleship." In the pithy language of stock-market analysts, Bush's new strategy may turn out to be a "dead cat bounce." (This refers to a brief market rally that occurs after the market crashes, to be followed by a further decline.) George W. Bush, who never wanted the Iraq mission to be compared to Vietnam, is now following faithfully in the footsteps of Richard Nixon. Nixon escalated the war in Southeast Asia to prepare the conditions for U.S. withdrawal. Bush began to do the same thing in Iraq. Perhaps this was a nod to his historical legacy. He aspired to leave the White House before the whole rotten structure that he had created in Iraq comes crashing down. Then, when someone came to ghostwrite his memoirs, Bush could claim that he did not cut and run. He would be able to leave that sorry chapter to his successor.

What became abundantly clear, though, was that the United States was no longer committed to winning the fight in Iraq. What is at issue now is the withdrawal strategy. All the talk about building a democracy in Iraq has been so much hot air. Soon no-one but historians will pay any attention to it.

Bush's policy of sending reinforcements to Iraq amounted to a rejection of the recommendations of the Iraq Study Group. It also flew in the face of the message that American voters sent when they handed both houses of Congress to the Democrats in the November 2006 elections.

The Bush White House, however, had lost much of its freedom to set U.S. policy. The Iraq reinforcement had now to be couched in terms of the goal of bringing American troops home. That being the case, what we are witnessing is the beginning of the American "end game" in the Iraq conflict. The chances of the current Iraq government surviving into even the middle-term future are remote. As the Americans prepare to leave, the country may disintegrate into its constituent parts. If that were to occur, the paramount U.S. and Western interest would be to maintain their hold on Iraqi petroleum. The Americans could well end up pulling their forces out of Iraq, or most of it, and setting up a large and permanent presence in Kuwait from which they can oversee the petroleum reserves of the Persian Gulf region. That could be the course of political realism as the neo-conservative fantasies about remaking the Middle East in the American image evaporate.

Baker and Hamilton and the other members of the Study Group have not lost the battle to reset American Middle East policy. Their views are in the ascendancy with the American political elites and the American people. The realists, for their part, watched the Bush administration lead the United States down the path to disaster in the two wars it launched. They have no appetite for a further war against Iran, seeing this as potentially leading to an even greater disaster. They prefer a tough set of negotiations with Teheran and Damascus and a deal that will ensure the paramount position of the United States in the region.

The present period in the United States should be seen as an interregnum. The age of neo-conservative control of policy-making has ended, but it is not fully clear what will come next.

The jockeying for position among the presidential hopefuls for 2008 in both the Republican and Democratic camps took shape around the Iraq question. The debate has two focal points. The first concerns the positions taken by candidates in the October 2002 vote in the U.S. Senate authorizing Bush to use force if necessary to strip Saddam Hussein of his weapons of mass destruction. The second is the position taken by presidential candidates on the way to end the war and bring the troops home.

The U.S. Senate vote in October 2002 was later used by the Bush administration as authorization for its March 2003 invasion of Iraq. The vote has already played a pivotal role in shaping perceptions of heavyweight U.S. senators. John Kerry, for instance, voted for the resolution, declaring his support for the proposition that it could become necessary to use force to strip the Iraqi dictator of his weapons of mass destruction. After the invasion, when it was revealed that Iraq had possessed no weapons of mass destruction, Kerry denounced Bush for having misled the country. He repudiated his 2002 vote in the Senate. That change of position was used with effect by Republicans during the 2004 presidential campaign to portray the Democratic standard-bearer as a flip-flop artist. Two other Democratic senators with presidential aspirations for 2008 also voted for the 2002 resolution: John Edwards and Hillary Clinton. Edwards has since repudiated his 2002 vote and began playing a leading role in denouncing Bush's strategy in Iraq. Clinton has been more cautious. She did not go so far as to repudiate her Senate vote, merely noting that if Americans knew then what they later learned, there would have been no such vote.

On the Republican side, John McCain, vying for his party's 2008 nomination, voted for the 2002 resolution and stands staunchly behind that vote.

On the second focal issue, the way to wind up the war, the presidential hopefuls have also engaged in jockeying for position. In mid-January 2007 Clinton flew to Baghdad, where she met with Iraqi prime minister Nuri Kamal al-Maliki. While she had previously said that she did not back the Bush administration's surge strategy, she remained vague about where she stood, saying she would have more to say later. Her unwillingness to distance herself more sharply from the war and the administration led many Democrats to become disillusioned with her as a presidential candidate. Polls revealed that only one in four Americans were now supporting Bush on the Iraq war.

Among Republicans, McCain defines himself as the hawk's hawk. I remember hearing him speak at an outdoor rally in Rochester, New York, in March 2000 during the campaign for his party's nomination. A Vietnam veteran, McCain declared that what he had learned from that conflict was that the United States should never go to war again without the willingness to do everything necessary to prevail. He has stuck to that position ever since. While he backs Bush on the war, he believes the United States should have sent a much larger number of additional troops. The position that McCain staked out on the war would have a strong effect on his fate in the run for the Republican nomination. For hard-core Republicans, who regard McCain as soft on social issues, his staunch support of the war has won him friends. The problem for him is that the country as a whole is negative about the war, and that includes some high-profile Republicans. Senator Chuck Hagel of Nebraska, also a Vietnam veteran, has long since become a critic of Bush's handling of the war. Senator Sam Brownback of Kansas has repudiated the Bush administration's decision to send additional troops to Iraq.

While travelling in Iraq in January 2007, Brownback said that he did not believe that sending more troops was the answer. "Iraq requires a political rather than a military solution," he said. Following meetings with the Iraqi prime minister, the Kansas senator said he did not think that the United States should increase its involvement in Iraq until Sunnis and Shiites stopped "shooting at each other." While Brownback supported the war in the past, he began to move away from administration positions. He called for the division of Iraq into autonomous Kurdish, Sunni, and Shiite regions within a loosely configured federation. He declared that he generally supported the approach of the Iraq Study Group.

The U.S. position on the Iraq war is shifting rapidly, and those supporting Bush are becoming ever weaker and more defensive. When the debate shifts to Afghanistan, the same dynamics will be at work.

■ ■

10

Bringing Canadian Troops Home

CANADIANS HAVE EVERY RIGHT TO BE SCEPTICAL, AT THE very least, about the war in Afghanistan. The Canadian mission in Afghanistan has never been as advertised.

Apparently a straightforward fight against terrorism on behalf of human rights, the realities of the mission have been shrouded in deception from the very start. Initially, in the autumn of 2001, the announcement of the mission was a way for the Chrétien government, with its tense relationship with the Bush administration, to express solidarity with the Americans in the aftermath of the September 11 attacks. The members of the Chrétien cabinet undoubtedly thought the conflict would be of brief duration and that the Canadian role in it would be unimportant. By March 2003, when the United States invaded Iraq, it was clear that the Afghan mission would be lasting longer than originally anticipated.

Chrétien's refusal to join the "coalition of the willing" in Iraq, the most popular decision he ever made as prime minister, put Ottawa more at odds than ever with Washington. The Canadian mission in Afghanistan then became a back-door means through which Chrétien could assure the Bush administration that Canada was doing its part in the broader War on Terror. The short-lived government of Paul Martin further adjusted the focus on Afghanistan when it signalled its willingness to deploy more Canadians in the south of the country, the zone of heavy fighting. For the Martin government, this move, along with a shift to a more pro-Israeli stance in the Middle East, was a way of cozying up to Washington.

When the Harper Conservatives won their minority election victory in January 2006, the politics of Canada's Afghan mission altered yet again. While in opposition, Harper made it clear that he thought Canada should enter the fray in Iraq. As the leader of a shaky minority government, however, at a time when Canadians were solidly opposed to participation in the Iraq war, Harper found a new use for the Afghanistan mission. It became his way to signal his neo-conservative bona fides both to the Bush administration and to his core right-wing base in Canada. Unlike the Liberals, who were wary of Washington, Harper was genuinely and fervently pro-American. Harper expressed the view that Canada's casualties in Afghanistan were the price the country had to pay for greater influence in global affairs.

While the politics of the Afghanistan war for Canadian governments has been a shifting game of smoke and mirrors, the consequences of that game have been very real. On a per capita basis Canadians have suffered more casualties in the conflict than have any other countries sending troops to participate. That this outcome should have been visited upon Canada and Canadians, and particularly on those

Canadians who have been killed or wounded, has been a tragic result of a political process that has never been transparent. Canadians have been poorly served by the Chrétien, Martin, and Harper governments on the Afghanistan question.

The war in Afghanistan, like the struggle in Iraq, is doing more to promote the cause of terrorism throughout the Islamic world than it is doing to win the so-called War on Terror. The argument made by some that to advocate withdrawal is appeasement and that we have a choice between fighting this enemy in Asia or on our own doorstep is a completely phony one.

Like previous invasions of Afghanistan, this intervention is almost certain to end in failure. Eventually the West will decide to pull its troops out, leaving an even more despoiled country to sort itself out. The values touted by the West—democracy, human rights, and equality for women—are considered by many in Afghanistan and in other parts of the Middle East and Central Asia as nothing more than the crusader myths of outside invaders. The causes that we hold most dear are being sullied in this war.

Canada is not a great power, and has no strategic interests in Central Asia. It is time for this country to signal to its NATO allies our intention to pull our troops out of Afghanistan, giving them reasonable notice of our decision. Withdrawing from Afghanistan will enable Canada to pursue a more independent foreign policy—a policy not hopelessly compromised by support for the failing global policies of the U.S. government.

The European effort in Afghanistan has been grudging from the start. When the strategic policy in Washington shifts, as it promises to do, and Afghanistan falls into obscurity, the Europeans will be happy to pick up and go home. They will not be offended by a Canadian decision to do the same.

What will we owe the Afghans as we withdraw our military forces? Apart from an explanation as to why we came and decided to leave, we owe that country continued economic assistance, in addition to programs tailored to training and educating Afghans in Canada, to help in the reconstruction of their country. The Canadian government has insisted from the very start that the mission in Afghanistan is divided into two crucial components: military and reconstruction aid. But the military side of the mission has received 90 per cent of the funding. That imbalance ought to be redressed as we pull our military force out of Afghanistan. It should be Canada's policy to provide aid to the people of Afghanistan up to the level that we have spent on the military mission. The amount would depend on when we end the military operation there, but at present this approach would mean that Canada would provide at least $3.5 billion in additional aid over a period of five or six years.

■ ■

11

Towards a New Canadian Foreign Policy

FOR CANADIANS, THE AFGHANISTAN OPERATION HAS BEEN a mission of folly. Canada blindly followed the United States into a war that is not winnable, a war from which no positive results can be anticipated. Now that American public opinion has turned sharply against the war in Iraq, U.S. involvement in Afghanistan will not long endure. Americans will move on to other engagements, other power struggles, and new priorities. By the time the Bush administration is out of office, the chances are that the Afghanistan mission will be on its last legs.

As Americans pursue a modified foreign policy, the opportunity opens for Canada to chart its own course in the world. In recent years, it has become commonplace for critics on the political right to decry Canada's waning global influence. Those critics have called on Canada to rearm and reassert itself alongside its military allies.

What these critics really want is for Canada to line up solidly with the United States, United Kingdom, and Australia to make a fourth in the "Anglo-Sphere."[1] With Afghanistan these critics got their way.

Canada took its place in the Anglo-Sphere in a shooting war, and Canadians have suffered their most serious military casualties since the Korean conflict. For Stephen Harper, who observed that these casualties were the price of greater global influence, this made sense.

In truth, however, Canada's global influence has not been increasing. If anything, it has been diminishing. In Afghanistan Canada has been engaged in a hopeless American adventure. In the Middle East Canada has aligned itself so closely with Israel that we have stripped our country of whatever small influence it formerly had. Canada's pursuit of influence in the military adventures of the Anglo-Sphere has proved to be a dead end.

Canadians need to think through the principles on which a new Canadian foreign policy should rest. Although discussions of Canadian foreign policy often skirt around the principle of furthering our domestic interests in the international sphere, that should be the starting point for any foreign policy; a second goal should be to advance the principles to which Canada is committed in the wider world. These two goals are not necessarily contradictory.

Canada's vital national interests have always been much easier to spell out than to realize. That's what comes of living in a unique neighbourhood in which an otherwise potentially influential country is left feeling quite impotent because it is located next door to the world's only superpower. The power imbalance between Canada and its puissant neighbour has always made Canadian foreign policy a peculiar amalgam of resignation and utopianism.

On the resignation side, a species of lobbyists whom I would call "continentalists in realist clothing" have argued that Canada cannot challenge the wishes of the United States on fundamental issues and that its best course of action is to accommodate to the direction that America is determined to take and to obtain the greatest influence and the best bargain in the process. In 1964 a former U.S. ambassador to Ottawa and a former Canadian ambassador to Washington collaborated to write a report (Merchant-Heeney Report) that set out this approach. The report called on Canada to negotiate vigorously with the United States on bilateral issues, but to recognize the special global role of the United States. On wider international questions, therefore, where Canada disagreed with U.S. policies, Ottawa ought to pursue what the report called "quiet diplomacy." Canada ought to refrain from public disagreements with the United States on global issues that did not directly concern Canadian interests. The Merchant-Heeney Report quickly became notorious because it recommended what most people saw as an unacceptable abandonment of Canadian sovereignty, an unnecessary acceptance of U.S. suzerainty on global issues.

While Ottawa did not adopt that report, over the past four decades the approach that it advocated has been advanced repeatedly in one form or another by pro-U.S. lobby groups. The C.D. Howe Institute, Fraser Institute, and Canadian Council of Chief Executives (formerly Business Council on National Issues) have tirelessly promoted the notion that Canadian foreign and defence policies should be closely co-ordinated with those of Washington. In his maiden speech in the House of Commons as leader of the opposition in May 2002, Harper, then leader of the Canadian Alliance, excoriated the record of the Liberal government on the issue of Canadian-American relations. He accused the Liberals of having undermined the relationship with

Washington by taking holier than thou positions on issues such as the treaty banning the use of land mines. He concluded that anything that substantially harmed the United States would devastate Canada.

His speech is worth quoting at some length because it provides such a clear statement of the continentalist position:

> Downright hostility to the United States, anti-Americanism, has come to characterize other elements of Canadian policy. In 1996–97 Canada aggressively pushed forward the treaty to ban land mines without giving due consideration to U.S. concerns about potential implications for its security forces in South Korea. What did we end up with? We ended up with a ban on land mines that few major land mine producers or users have signed.
>
> Most recently we have been inclined to offer knee-jerk resistance to the United States on national missile defence despite the fact that Canada is confronted by the same threats from rogue nations equipped with ballistic missiles and weapons of mass destruction as is the United States....
>
> The government has not adequately addressed the matter of security in the context of continental security. Because of the unreformed nature of our refugee determination system, we continue to be subject to unique internal security and continental security dangers.[2]

Having dismissed Chrétien as a leader who was always anti-free trade, Harper commended Brian Mulroney for having "understood a fundamental truth. He understood that mature and intelligent

Canadian leaders must share the following perspective: the United States is our closest neighbour, our best ally, our biggest customer and our most consistent friend."

He concluded: "Not only does the United States have this special relationship to us, it is the world leader when it comes to freedom and democracy.... If the United States prospers, we prosper. If the United States hurts or is angry, we will be hurt. If it is ever broadly attacked, we will surely be destroyed."

Adherents of the continentalist school of thought, of which Harper is a charter member, make the case that on important military questions Canada has no choice but to align itself with the United States. Historian Jack Granatstein advanced this argument in a study for the C.D. Howe Institute several years ago. We can label this the "continentalist school of Canadian foreign policy." Its essential tenet is that Canada is an eco-nomic, political, cultural, and military extension of the United States, a lesser power whose larger fate is bound up with that of its neighbour. This school of thought was enormously influential in its advocacy of the Canada–U.S. Free Trade Agreement in the 1980s and the North Amer-ican Free Trade Agreement (NAFTA) in the 1990s. In recent decades the members of the continentalist school have been the most consistent advocates of a coherent approach to Canadian foreign policy.

Over the course of Canadian history there have been other coherent approaches. From the time of Confederation in 1867 until the Second World War, the dominant school of Canadian foreign policy was what might be called "imperial-nationalist." At the beginning of this historical period, of course, Canadian foreign and military policies were legally in the hands of Westminster, although Canada had control of its domestic affairs. This makes the term foreign policy premature and, indeed, for decades the Canadian foreign ministry was called the Department of External Affairs. The great architect of the imperial-nationalist school was John A. Macdonald, Canada's first prime minister. His Tory-nationalism was the ideology that suffused the Canadian state and its economic policies for many decades.

The imperial-nationalist approach to foreign or external affairs grew out of the proposition that the supreme threat to Canadian nationhood arose not from Canada's colonial relationship with Britain, but from Canada's uneasy position vis-à-vis the United States. Macdonald believed that Canada needed Britain to offset the threat from the south. During the Second World War, the policy of British prime minister Winston Churchill was to call on the power of the New World to redress the balance in the Old. Macdonald's policy was the reverse of that: he called on the power of the Old World to redress the balance in the New.

The Second World War destroyed the power relations in the North Atlantic on which the imperial-nationalist school was based. The British Empire disintegrated in the years following the war, and the American Empire took its place. Canada could no longer seek a balance in its relationships with the two great English-speaking powers. Britain's decline spelt the end of the imperial-nationalist school of Canadian foreign policy. Still, the sentiments on which the school had rested outlived the disappearance of the geopolitical basis for the implementation of its policies.

Nationalist conservatism has remained a significant sentiment in Canada, but as neo-conservatism grew the tendency lost its traditional home in the Progressive Conservative Party. Today's Conservative Party of Canada is firmly locked within the logic of the continentalist school of Canadian foreign policy.

Over the past four decades, as political and cultural movements have arisen to contest the degree of U.S. domination of Canada, the basis for a new school of Canadian foreign policy has emerged. We can call it the "Canadian school."

The Canadian school seeks to achieve two large goals. The first is to promote the survival of Canada as a sovereign power in North America. The second is to promote in the wider world the values to which Canadians are committed. The first goal grows directly out of Canadian domestic policies. Canadians who have embraced their nation's potential as something far greater than the quest for immediate material gratification will appreciate that our country has the capacity to enlarge itself in human terms over the course of this century. Americans in the nineteenth century perceived their country's potential to achieve more in the future than it had in the past. Canadians—at least those not bounded by the limiting confines of neo-conservatism and the subservience of the continentalist school of Canadian foreign policy—realize that they are creating a country that will be greater in the future than it is today. The present generation of Canadians has, then, an immense responsibility to pursue the interests of Canada today in a way that does not foreclose on the potential of the country for the future.

For the present, Canada needs a foreign policy with one eye on the long-term future, and the other on the present. The mixture needed is one that combines realism with a dose of utopianism. The Canada to come over the course of this century can expect to play as large a role in the world as the United Kingdom or France does. Consider the record of

the past century. At the beginning of the twentieth century, with a population of five million, Canada was 5 per cent as populous as the United
States. When the century closed, Canada was more than 10 per cent
as populous as its southern neighbour. Wilfrid Laurier's boast that the
"twentieth century belongs to Canada" has always seemed more than a
little over the top, but he was not entirely wrong. During the twentieth
century both Canada's population and its economy more than doubled
in size relative to the population and economy of the United States.
Reluctant and non-visionary though the country's leadership has often
been, Canada has thrived over the course of the past hundred years.

Like the British Empire of the nineteenth century, Canada has
grown in a fit of absence of mind. For our good fortune to continue,
however, a more concerted approach is needed. The Canadian school
needs to drive home the point that the continentalist school is guilty of
taking an extremely short-term approach, and of not even doing a good
job of that. The curious thing about the Canadian business lobbyists,
for whom the continentalist school speaks, is how lacking in serious
ambition they are. Living as they do on a piece of real estate that is
among the greatest on earth, and that is inhabited by a population that
is highly motivated and well educated, you would think that Canadian
business lobbyists would aspire to more than playing second fiddle to
the Americans. One might imagine that Canadian business would want
real power for itself, willing to engage in commerce with whomever
but always realizing that they could occupy a larger place in the global
scheme of things. In the nineteenth century, U.S. business moguls had
that sense of themselves. John D. Rockefeller, the founder of Standard
Oil and the world's first billionaire, built his global petroleum empire

through a peculiar combination of cutthroat competition and Christian piety. He was seriously religious and believed in a social Darwinist business ethic in which the stronger prevailed and the weak perished. Standard Oil set its sights on the domination, not only of the American petroleum market, but also of the global market.

The Rockefeller story has been repeated many times over in the annals of American business, right down to the present epics of the Waltons and Bill Gates. By contrast, Canadian business moguls have usually been full of bluster but highly derivative in their ambitions, wanting little more for themselves than acceptance from their British and U.S. counterparts. The consequence is that they have been quite prepared to concede the genuine power that could have been theirs in return for a comfortable seat in someone else's vehicle.

Under the circumstances, an alternative vision of Canada's place in the world and its foreign policy will have to be based on other social forces. At first glance this may seem to be a rather dim prospect, but there are reasons for hope. For several decades Canada has been that odd case, a country whose population has grown ever more committed to its survival in the face of business spokespersons who have largely abandoned this cause.

The collapse of the Bush administration's strategy in the Middle East and Central Asia makes the prospects for a shift in Canadian foreign policy brighter. Those who have been most inclined to follow the Bush line in Canada—the Harper Conservatives and the business lobbyists—have damaged their cause immeasurably in their stolid adherence to the lost cause. Theirs will be the fate of spear carriers through the ages who have wound up on the wrong side.

The new Canadian foreign policy should aim at preserving Canadian sovereignty and on lending Canada's weight in the world to greater political and economic justice and environmental sustainability. Canadians need to recognize that in the world of the twenty-first century, national sovereignty is an immeasurably valuable asset. The American novelist Mark Twain once advised people to buy land on the grounds that "they're not making anymore of that." The same thing is basically true when it comes to sovereign nations. It is true that a rash of them became sovereign in the great age of decolonization in the several decades following the Second World War. Then there was a second rash following the breakup of the Soviet Union; and Yugoslavia and Czechoslovakia were dismantled.

But the point stands. Not many new sovereign states will be created over the course of the present century. Those that exist will prize their sovereignty as an asset that gives them admission to international decision-making bodies and that allows them to shape affairs on their own territory to a considerable extent.

These assertions fly in the face of much received wisdom in the so-called age of globalization. With the fall of the Soviet Empire, the world entered the brief era of the supposed End of History and the Borderless World. The curtain rang down on that brief epoch on September 11, 2001. The terror attacks were followed by the rediscovery of the state—in fact, it had never gone away. The American state, which presided over the greatest empire of our time, under the direction of the Bush administration, staked its claim to remaining the world's paramount military power in permanence. The contradiction at the heart of the American Empire was that while it was able to shape the course of politics, the economy, and society in many countries, it relied on the state apparatus in each country to administer affairs locally.

The great fact of our age is that we live in a world dominated by the American Empire, but it is a world in which the sovereign state is increasingly valued as a priceless asset by peoples everywhere. Empire and nationalism co-exist today as they co-existed in the age of the great European empires.

In the new age, while Canadians have had very little leadership on this score from political leaders or intellectuals, they have moved in the same direction as other peoples in cherishing the survival of their state. Canadians have had a curious history on the question of national sovereignty in recent years. From the political right, once a strong source of support for a sovereign Canada distinct from the United States, Canadians now receive continentalist rhetoric, buoyed up by neo-conservative notions that the strong state is anathema to a free people. Neo-conservative ideas propel Canada towards descent into a series of regional extensions of the United States, tethered together by a weak federal government.

On the political left, the tradition of left nationalism has been strong and has had a major cultural impact. Left nationalism propelled the campaigns against the supine acceptance of American corporate ownership of the Canadian economy and played a seminal role in the resistance to free trade.

In recent years, however, other voices on the left have been far less concerned with national sovereignty. Some of these voices have been highly derivative of the ideas of the U.S.-centred anti-globalization movement. For them, the compelling questions in the world turn on the relationship of the rich nations of the North to the poor nations of the world. Canada's struggles to maintain its sovereignty vis-à-vis the United States have meant little to those with this point of view. Intellectually, in any case, they remained enamoured of the liberal anti-state ideologies that flourished during the brief post-Cold War era. Ironically, where the state is concerned, they shared much in common with neo-conservatives.

Those who believe that Canadian sovereignty needs to be sustained and extended should establish a set of goals.

If a major objective of Canadian foreign policy should be to foster a sustainable global environment, Canada will have to reacquire sovereignty in the critical area of the petroleum industry. Under the terms of NAFTA, at any given time Canada must continue to maintain petroleum exports to the United States at the average level of the preceding three years. In the event of a global petroleum crisis, should the supply of imported petroleum for Eastern Canada be interrupted, Canada is committed under NAFTA to meet its export commitments to the United States even if that means Eastern Canada would have to do without. (Mexico, on the other hand, also a major exporter of petroleum to the United States, is subject to no such commitment under NAFTA.)

As conventional Canadian oil production declines, Canada is becoming ever more reliant on oil sands production to sustain and increase overall petroleum output. Utilizing present production methods, which involve the use of enormous quantities of fresh water, large-scale strip mining, the injection of clean natural gas to produce oil from the sands, and the emission of a huge volume of greenhouse gases, increasing oil sands production condemns Canada to a dirty global environmental role.

For Canada to achieve its environmental objectives, at home and abroad, the present U.S. lock on the oil sands has to be broken. This will require either an amendment to NAFTA, to remove the Canadian requirement to supply the United States with petroleum, or the abrogation by Canada of its place in that treaty. Withdrawing from NAFTA would position Canada within the trade regulations of the World Trade Organization. Those who fear that leaving NAFTA would place Canada in the line of fire for U.S. retaliation should keep in mind the backup of the regulations of the World Trade Organization.

Other crucial goals need to be addressed as elements of Canada's bilateral foreign policy with the United States. Recognized as important by successive Conservative and Liberal governments, but with little action to back it up, is the need to sustain Canada's claim to its Arctic territorial waters. The United States, Russia, and the European Union refuse to accept Canada's claim to the Northwest Passage as Canadian waters. The Harper government briefly toyed with the idea of spending serious money on the acquisition of ships to patrol our Arctic waters, but dropped the idea in favour of other military priorities. Constructing an Arctic patrol fleet should be the first new military undertaking in line with a new foreign policy. In autumn 2007 representatives of the Harper government again raised the question of Arctic sovereignty, as a way of appealing to nationalist sentiment, without making any real commitment to doing anything about it.

Sovereignty also requires Canada to halt and reverse steps towards the concept of a Fortress North America alongside the United

States. Canadian refugee and immigration policies should be de-linked from those of Washington. In the past, linking refugee policies to those of the United States would have resulted in consequences most Canadians would have lamented. After the U.S.-backed coup in Chile in 1973, thousands of refugees were admitted to Canada. A refugee policy linked to that of Washington would have prevented those Chileans from reaching solace and a new life in Canada.

Canada should also halt the move towards the interoperability of Canadian with U.S. military units. Interoperability is not a technical matter, although it is often portrayed that way. It is a political choice. The assumption underlying it is that Canada's main military operations will be alongside the Americans or, more accurately, under U.S. command. The premise of an alternative foreign policy is that Canada's first military priority should be to patrol the nation's territorial waters, especially those in the Arctic. It flies in the face of elementary logic for a country to integrate its armed forces with those of a country with which it has an ongoing, indeed deepening, dispute over territorial sovereignty. Would the Americans integrate their armed forces with those of a state that disputes Washington's claim to an important portion of U.S. territory?

The second priority of the Canadian military, which also does not require interoperability with U.S. forces, should be to prepare for participation in international missions that fall under the heading of the "Responsibility to Protect," a principle recognized by the United Nations as an international obligation. The Responsibility to Protect arises when peoples face catastrophes, whether natural or human-made. The tsunami in South Asia in December 2004 is an example of the former. The Rwandan genocide and the ethnic cleansing in Sudan are examples of the latter.

Is it possible in a world dominated by the United States, and its potential challengers, most notably China, to find ways of addressing humanitarian catastrophes that are not bound to end up simply opening the way for the achievement of imperial aims? In the twenty-first century, is humanitarian intervention nothing more than the equivalent of missionary efforts in the nineteenth and early twentieth centuries—efforts that provided a fig leaf for imperial aggression? Must we face the hard truth that humanitarian interventions cannot be conceived in good faith until empires have been reconciled with nation-states and international law? And will this predicament become worse as the American Empire faces increasing challenges from China and other actors over the next twenty or thirty years?

If those who would rely on the American Empire to deliver aid to suffering people do not have the answer, two other possibilities remain: reform of the global system from above; or transformation of the system from below. Should reform from above prove a failure, as well it might, that leaves transformation from below as the road ahead. Uncertain, uneven, and explosive, upheaval from below will erupt in those cases in which poverty, exploitation, and authoritarianism, as well as ethnic and religious oppression, can be effectively countered by force. Where and when such volcanic eruptions may occur in Latin America, and parts of Africa and Asia, the one certainty is that the consequences will not be those that warm the hearts of liberal democrats, with their preference for pluralism, the rule of law, civil liberties, and fair elections.

What, then, of reform from above?

Efforts at transforming the United Nations have been undertaken many times in the past, and almost always with meagre results. More often than not what has stood in the way of reform is the unwillingness of member states to cede power in a way that makes the UN more of a supranational authority and less of an intergovernmental organization. The five permanent members of the Security Council (P5), armed with vetoes, have always been, and remain today, jealous of the clout the veto gives them. On top of this, the United States, with its unique power, has shown its unwillingness to submit to any international regime or regulation that it sees as threatening its right to control its security and retain its full sovereignty.

One could conclude that that is the end of the matter.

At present, initiatives to reform the UN to enable it to be much more effective in delivering humanitarian aid are being seriously pursued in a number of places. Let us explore one possible way forward.

When it comes to potential actors, hope lies with a number of countries that are relatively wealthy, but that lack the capacity, military and economic, to vie for global power. What is needed is a system for undertaking humanitarian interventions that is as insulated as possible from imperial power rivalries. Of course, perfection in this regard is unattainable. Let's concede, at once, some of the limitations. Humanitarian interventions are not possible in areas that are directly controlled by great imperial states (for example, Tibet, or Panama or Colombia). They are also not likely to be possible in zones in which rival imperial powers are in active contention with each other.

In other cases, however, it could be possible to launch a system, under the auspices of the United Nations, in which the notion of the

Responsibility to Protect can be acted on in clearly defined cases of humanitarian catastrophe. Second-tier countries, while often closely tied to imperial powers—as Canada is to the United States—also have their own interests and aspirations, which include a desire not to be completely subsumed within the *weltanschauung* of the world power. It is worth investigating the proposition that an international role for such countries as purveyors of humanitarian interventions, acting through UN mandates under the rubric of the Responsibility to Protect, could be established. For such countries to invest their treasure and their manpower in these missions would carve out a significant global role for them. Further, it would, in many cases at least, remove the taint of imperial aggression from such interventions.

No-one ought to contend that such missions would much reduce the spheres of imperial power in the world. Indeed, such a role for second-tier states would deal with situations that the United States and the other imperial powers would rather avoid. This point is crucial, because it means that a space could be found for action that does not imply a direct confrontation with the power of the United States and its major competitors.

What countries falling under the heading of second-tier could be recruited to play such a role? The criteria for inclusion could be broad. First, there ought to be a crucial restriction. The list should not include powers that possess nuclear weapons. Obvious candidates for the list would include Canada, the Scandinavian countries, the Netherlands, Belgium, Spain, Australia, and New Zealand. Poland, the Czech Republic, Italy, Mexico, Brazil, South Korea, and South Africa could qualify. More controversial would be Germany and Japan.

What could emerge from this sort of initiative could be a new layer of power directed at alleviating humanitarian crises. This international mission could reduce human suffering and, arguably, contribute to a safer world.

In conjunction with a Canadian commitment to enlarging the capacity of this country and others to act under the UN rubric of the Responsibility to Protect, Canada ought to move swiftly to providing 0.7 per cent of its Gross Domestic Product for Official Development Assistance. This goal, first included in 1970 in a UN General Assembly resolution as a target towards which developed countries should move, has for far too long been evaded by successive Canadian governments.

■ ■

The Afghanistan mission, conceived with little thought, has taught an important, if costly, lesson about the falseness of seeking to enhance Canada's global position through participation in the armed struggles of the countries that make up the Anglo-Sphere. Even though Canadians have paid a disproportionately high price in blood in Afghanistan in relation to that paid by our allies, the country has seen no increase in its influence on other nations. In the wider world, the effect of the Harper government's foreign policy has been to reinforce one perception of Canadians that is already strongly held—that we amount to little more than an extension of the United States in thought and in action.

That is highly unfortunate, because another perception of Canada has been taking hold in the wider world in recent decades. That perception is of a country that is genuinely a refuge of liberty and tolerance, a human space in which the world's travails can be addressed in a calm and compassionate way.

In the narrower world of the Anglo-Sphere, the consequences of the Harper government's foreign policy have been telling, and not a little ironic. In Afghanistan Canada measured up to the standards of sacrifice of the Americans and the British, but the impact on Washington and London has been negligible. On softwood lumber, Washington pushed a completely self-interested bargain on Canada, taking no account at all of "Steve" being at the helm in Ottawa. On the Mahar Arar case, the Bush administration refused to take the Syrian-born Canadian off its watch list despite the request from the Harper government that they do so in the aftermath of an exhaustive Canadian investigation. The much-touted friendship between Secretary of State Condoleezza Rice and Foreign Affairs Minister Peter MacKay meant nothing when the chips were down.

As for wider public opinion in the United States and Britain, Canadian casualties were simply not noticed by the American and British media, which were no more inclined to cover Canada after the sacrifices than before. As it has turned out, the supposed realism preached by Canadian neo-conservatives has produced no tangible benefits for this country.

Surely the time has come to turn the page and move on—to stake out a foreign policy rooted not just in self-interest but also in the quest for a better world, the combination that is sorely needed in a country whose best days are in the future.

■ ■

Notes

1. CANADA IN AFGHANISTAN: WAR FIRST, RATIONALE LATER

1. Canada, *House of Commons Debates*, Ottawa, March 17, 2003.
2. Ibid., March 25, 2003.
3. *The Globe and Mail*, May 17, 2006.
4. "Europeans, Canadians, See Afghan Mission as Failure," Angus Reid Global Monitor, August 27, 2007; Brian Laghi, "Anxiety Grows about Economy, Jobs, Poll Finds," *The Globe and Mail*, January 15, 2008, p.A4.
5. Brian Laghi and Alan Freeman, "PM's Choice of Manley Catches Liberals Off Guard," *The Globe and Mail*, October 13, 2007, p.A1.

2. THE INVASION AND OCCUPATION

1. Globalsecurity.org.
2. Whitehouse.gov.
3. Guardian Unlimited, October 7, 2001.
4. CBC Archives.
5. *The Globe and Mail*, May 2, 2003.
6. Washingtonpost.com, December 6, 2007.
7. *The Observer*, November 18, 2001.
8. PBS.org.
9. Cooperativeresearch.org.
10. BBC News, December 7, 2004.
11. Medscape.com.
12. Globalsecurity.org.
13. BBC News, October 12, 2001.
14. *The Guardian*, October 23, 2001.
15. *Boston Globe*, December 2, 2001.
16. BBC News, July 1, 2002.
17. Globalsecurity.org.
18. Associated Press, January 20, 2004.
19. Foxnews.com, October 18, 2006.
20. BBC News, October 26, 2006.
21. CTV.ca, September 26, 2007.
22. *Washington Post*, November 18, 2007.

3. THE CANADIAN MISSION

1. Janice Gross Stein and Eugene Lang, *The Unexpected War: Canada in Kandahar* (Toronto: Viking Canada, 2007), p.1.
2. NATO.int., October 5, 2001.
3. CTV.ca.
4. NATO.int., December 10, 2007.
5. Stein and Lang, *Unexpected War*, p.11.
6. CBC News Online, June 6, 2005.
7. Canada, *House of Commons Debates*, February 12, 2003.
8. CTV.ca, February 10, 2005.
9. Ibid., June 29, 2005.
10. Ibid., July 16, 2005.
11. Ibid., February 25, 2006.
12. *The Guardian*, June 15, 2006.
13. CNN.com/world.
14. CTV.ca, October 6, 2006.
15. Ibid., October 6, 2006.
16. NDP.ca, August 31, 2006.
17. *Sunday Telegraph*, October 7, 2007.
18. CIDA News Release, March 31, 2004.
19. CBC News, May 17, 2006.
20. Ibid.

4. TO SUPPORT THE TROOPS, TAKE COVER BEHIND THEM

1. *The Toronto Star*, June 22, 2007.
2. *Ibid.*, June 14, 2007.
3. CTV.ca, June 22, 2007.
4. Canoe.ca, June 20, 2007.
5. *The Globe and Mail*, June 20, 2007.

6. *Ibid.*, June 23, 2007.
7. CBC Sports, July 10, 2007.
8. CTV.ca, August 24, 2007.
9. DND.ca.
10. *Ottawa Citizen*, September 2, 2007.
11. CTV.ca, May 2, 2007.

**5. THE MANY INVASIONS
OF AFGHANISTAN**

1. For an overview of the British presence in Afghanistan, see Denis Judd, *Empire: The British Imperial Experience from 1765 to the Present* (London: Phoenix, 2001).
2. For an overview of the Soviet invasion of Afghanistan and its aftermath, see M. Hassan Kakar, *Afghanistan: The Soviet Invasion and the Afghan Response, 1979–1982* (Berkeley: University of California Press, 1995).
3. CNN.com, March 31, 2001.

6. CANADA'S ALLIES

1. Angus Reid Global Monitor, August 27, 2007.

**7. PAKISTAN'S
DUPLICITOUS ROLE**

1. *Le Nouvel Observateur*, January 21, 1998.
2. Pervez Musharraf, *In the Line of Fire: A Memoir* (New York: Free Press, 2006).
3. CBS News, September 24, 2006.
4. *Ibid.*, September 24, 2006.
5. BBC News, October 6, 2007.
6. *The Guardian*, October 19, 2007.
7. BBC News, November 3, 2007.
8. CBC News, November 3, 2007.
9. *The Guardian*, November 6, 2007.

**8. THIS WAR IS NOT ABOUT
HUMAN RIGHTS**

1. Jon Lee Anderson, "The Taliban's Opium War," *The New Yorker*, July 9, 2007.
2. Guardian Unlimited, January 1, 2005.
3. Stein and Lang, *Unexpected War*, pp.249, 250.
4. Ibid., p.251.
5. *The Globe and Mail*, February 6, 2007.
6. Ibid., June 6, 2007.
7. Ibid., March 8, 2007.
8. Canada, *House of Commons Debates*, March 19, 2007.
9. *The Globe and Mail*, May 4, 2007.
10. Stein and Lang, *Unexpected War*, pp.257, 258.
11. Paul Koring and Alan Freeman, "Afghan Prisons: What Ottawa Knew," *The Globe and Mail*, November 16, 2007.
12. Human Rights Watch Backgrounder, October 2001.
13. Whitehouse.gov.
14. *Washington Post*, June 30, 2006.
15. Washingtonpost.com.
16. *The New York Times Magazine*, January 5, 2003; and *The New York Times Magazine*, August 5, 2007.
17. Thomas Friedman, *Longitudes and Attitudes: The World in the Age of Terrorism* (New York: Anchor Books, 2003), p.280.
18. Eric Margolis, *War at the Top of the World: The Struggle for Afghanistan and Asia* (Toronto: Key Porter Books, 2007).
19. *Toronto Sun*, April 2, 2006.

**9. THE UNITED STATES IS
LOSING THE WIDER WAR**

1. Newyorktimes.com.

2. Agence France Presse, October 2, 2007.
3. "Taliban Spokesman Rejects Karzai's Offer of Talks," CBC News, September 30, 2007; CBC.ca/world.
4. *The New York Times*, December 3, 2007.
5. *The Sunday Times* (London), January 7, 2007.
6. Whitehouse.gov.

11. TOWARDS A NEW CANADIAN FOREIGN POLICY

1. In November 2007 the defeat of John Howard's Liberal-National coalition at the hands of Kevin Rudd's Australian Labour Party blew a large hole in the unity of the Anglo-Sphere.
2. Canada, *House of Commons Debates*, May 28, 2002.

Index

INDEX